C. 1

MAR 3 1 1992			
SEP 0 8 1992			
AUG 1 2 1993			
AUG 2 1995			

HANK GREENBERG

Hall-of-Fame Slugger

HANK GREENBERG

Hall-of-Fame Slugger

IRA BERKOW

Illustrated by Mick Ellison

THE JEWISH PUBLICATION SOCIETY
Philadelphia—New York   5751 / 1991

Grateful acknowledgment is made to the following for permission to use
previously published material:
Contemporary Books, Inc.: "Speaking of Greenberg"
from Collected Verse of Edgar A. Guest, copyright © 1934.
Reprinted by arrangement with Contemporary Books, Inc., Chicago.
Reference photographs from the Estate of Henry Greenberg.
Reference photographs from The New York Times.
Reference photograph for jacket illustration courtesy of UPI/Bettmann
Newsphotos.

Library of Congress Cataloging-in-Publication Data
Berkow, Ira.
    Hank Greenberg : hall-of-fame slugger / Ira Berkow ; illustrated
by Mick Ellison.
        p.   cm.
    Includes index.
    Summary: A biography of the powerful home-run hitter who became
the first Jewish player elected to the Baseball Hall of Fame.
    ISBN 0–8276–0376–2 :
    1. Greenberg, Hank—Juvenile literature.   2. Baseball players—
United States—Biography—Juvenile literature.   3. Detroit Tigers
(Baseball team)—History—Juvenile literature.   [1. Greenberg,
Hank. 2. Baseball players. 3. Jews—Biography.]   I. Ellison,
Mick, ill. II. Title.
GV865.G68B47   1991
92—dc20
[796.357'092]
[B]   90–43005
                                                          CIP
                                                           AC

Book design by Adrianne Onderdonk Dudden

10 9 8 7 6 5 4 3 2 1

To Shayne

CONTENTS

ACKNOWLEDGMENT

The author wishes to acknowledge the kindness of the Greenberg family for use of material from the Estate of Hank Greenberg. He especially wants to express gratitude to Hank Greenberg's wife, Mary Jo Greenberg, and Hank's three children, Glenn Greenberg, Stephen Greenberg, and Alva Greenberg Gahagan.

INTRODUCTION

Hank Greenberg was often called the Jewish Babe Ruth. This son of Romanian immigrants became a powerful home-run hitter and the first truly outstanding Jewish baseball player in the "American Pastime." He eventually became the first Jewish player elected to the Baseball Hall of Fame.

Hank Greenberg, dark-haired and described in the press as "good-looking," stood six feet four and weighed over two hundred pounds. He became an idol for many Americans in every corner of the land, but he was especially honored by Jews.

When Greenberg was at his peak as a player, in the 1930s and 1940s, Jews frequently suffered discrimination in America, as well as in many other parts of the world. In America, Jews sometimes were abused, even physically, because of their religion or because they were born of Jewish parents. Sometimes there were anti-Semitic campaigns on radio and in newspapers. Some universities and businesses and even entire communities or neighborhoods were either closed to Jews or had Jewish quotas limiting the number of Jews they allowed in.

Greenberg, above all others in this time, represented the most visible example of a Jew as a high achiever, since baseball was so widely covered by the media, and so deeply loved by Americans.

"Hank Greenberg was the perfect standard bearer for Jews," said Shirley Povich, longtime sports columnist for the *Washington Post* and a Jew who covered Greenberg as a player. "He was smart, he was proud, and he was big!"

HANK GREENBERG

Hall-of-Fame Slugger

1

Boyhood in the Bronx

Hank Greenberg stood at the plate, his bat held high, the bill of his cap pulled low, the crowd in the big ballpark eager with anticipation. The pitcher wound up and threw. From left field, Ted Williams of the Boston Red Sox could see Greenberg, the number 5 of his Detroit Tiger uniform spread across his broad back. He watched him stride into the pitch, his bat coming around in a short, swift powerful stroke. And then Williams heard the crack of the distant bat.

"He had that nice rhythmic-y cut," recalled Williams years later, "not too hard, and he'd hit the ball to left when I was out there. The ball would start coming like you could make a play on it and then it would start going up! And up! It's in the upper deck!"

It was that swing that produced for Greenberg 331

home runs in his major-league career. He was among the all-time leaders when he retired, with 58 home runs in one season, 1938, when he came within two home runs of breaking Babe Ruth's famous record of 60. It was that swing that produced a home run with the bases loaded on the last day of the 1945 season to ensure the pennant for the Tigers, and it was that swing that produced hits and homers in four World Series.

No one, however, was even thinking about his swing, or baseball, when Hank Greenberg was born exactly forty-five minutes after the new year, at 12:45 A.M. on January 1, 1911. His family lived on the second floor of a six-floor walk-up on Barrow Street in Greenwich Village, a section of downtown New York City. The apartment buildings and the streets of the neighborhood teemed with people.

Barrow Street and later Perry Street, where Henry Benjamin Greenberg grew up, were populated mostly by Jewish immigrants from Europe. On neighboring streets lived other immigrant families of primarily Italian and Irish backgrounds.

Greenberg's parents, who spoke Yiddish and English, but mainly Yiddish at home, were orthodox Jews, observing religious holidays and customs, including keeping a kosher home. As a boy he attended services with his family on Friday nights and Saturday mornings.

Hank's father, David, believed that the best way for his children to grow up strong was with a particular diet, and that included milk and fruit. A snack consisted of milk and bread, and every dessert was an orange or an apple or, in summertime, a peach.

Baseball hardly existed in Greenwich Village. There

were no large areas, such as parks or schoolyards, where kids could romp and play baseball. They played stickball or some other game that could be managed on a city street. It was a tough neighborhood, and kids of one ethnic background took delight in beating up kids from another.

This led to another kind of game that involved Hank Greenberg. It took place every Halloween. Hank and his older brother and sister learned to stay home on that day. The reason was that in order to get to school, they had to pass from one end of the block to the other, and on Halloween that was dangerous.

The Italian and Irish kids would take the long black stockings that children wore in those days—along with their high-top shoes and knickers—and fill those stockings with what was supposed to be chalk. But often they left the chalk in the schoolroom and instead put ashes into the stockings, or sometimes even a rock or a solid piece of coal. And then the Italian and Irish kids, who often fought each other, called an armistice and went looking for Jewish kids to hit over the head with their stockings.

Jewish kids learned that the safest place for them on Halloween was home. And when they did venture out, Hank's mother, Sarah Greenberg, would warn her children: "Look out. Don't get the sock!"

Meanwhile, the neighborhood, from the viewpoint of Hank's parents, seemed to get even rowdier.

When Hank was seven years old, his family, as well as many other of the neighborhood's Jewish families, moved. Hank's dad had been doing reasonably well as the owner of a small fabric factory in lower Manhattan.

"Look out. Don't get the sock!"

He bought a three-story, ten-room home in the Bronx, another borough of New York City, several miles from the cramped, tough quarters of Greenwich Village.

The Bronx, with many open spaces, seemed like the country to young Hank. Though automobiles were becoming more popular in the nation, horses and wagons were still the general mode of transportation in the Bronx. Even street cars there were rare. But best of all, right across the street from the Greenberg house was a big, beautiful park named Crotona Park.

It was at Crotona Park that Hank learned to play baseball. More than that: He fell deeply and passionately in love with the game. He and his friends would pitch to each other and then shag, or run after, the balls that were hit to the outfield. Or they'd play "pepper." Pepper is a game in which several players stand about fifteen feet away from a batter and toss him a ball. He taps it back to them, helping him develop an "eye" for the ball, and helping the fielders improve their reflexes.

Every day as soon as school was out, Hank rushed to the park to play baseball. In summertime, he and his friends brought their lunch and played until dark. In winter, he even practiced his sliding in a pit that he made in the backyard, sometimes having to clear away the snow.

Not everyone appreciated the merits of the games. "Mrs. Greenberg has such nice children," some of the neighbors said. "Too bad one of them has to be a bum."

And Hank's mother wasn't thrilled either with her son spending so much time playing ball. "Why are you wasting your time playing baseball?" she would say. "It's a bum's game." His father warned that he would never make anything of himself. But the next day Hank would be back on the ball field.

They all thought that anyone who spent as much time at baseball as Hank would neglect his schoolwork. It turned out, however, that Hank was a good student with a good mind and, with the insistence of his parents, always did his homework.

His father worked hard and long hours, and his mother took care of the household chores. Hank and his brothers and sister were allowed a certain amount of freedom. There was Ben, who was four years older than Hank, and Lillian, who was two years older, and, soon, Joe, the last of the Greenberg children, who was five and a half years younger than Hank. As long as the kids stayed out of serious trouble and received passing grades in school, they had no problems at home.

Periodically, Hank was disciplined by his father in a way he would never forget. As Hank got a little older he also discovered another sport that he liked very much: basketball. And since he was growing tall, he began to excel at that sport. He played it a lot, especially in winter, in a recreation center near his home. The center closed at 9 P.M., and often Hank would come home with his shirt wet and try to sneak into the house. Sometimes with his homework assignment still untouched.

Sometimes his father caught him. Then Mr. Greenberg would take the strap out, and, as Hank recalled, "I'd get belted a few times."

It was also from an incident in basketball that Hank came by his nickname, one that would follow him through high school. One winter day he was playing a three-on-three basketball game outdoors in the park

8

when he got a little tired and said, "I'm groggy. I'm groggy." In some way, the word "groggy" got changed into "bruggy." Soon his friends were calling him "Bruggy." Years later, when he met people from his old neighborhood, they'd greet him with "hiya, Bruggy."

Hank, being from an orthodox family, became a bar-mitzvah at the age of thirteen. But as he got older, he, like many of his friends, drew away from strict observance of Jewish customs. He would debate with friends about various aspects of the Bible: what was the literal truth in it and what was strictly poetry? He began to question the merits of religion. Who is to say who knows what God is, who God is, and what God is thinking? He would continue to ask such questions for the rest of his life.

Hank entered James Monroe High School in the Bronx, where he continued to involve himself deeply in sports. He made all-city in soccer and basketball. He even played as an end in football in his senior year. He scored the decisive touchdown after catching a pass in the last game of the season against Monroe's archrival, George Washington High School. Hank, who by then had grown to six feet three, didn't care for football because he thought it wasn't a sport of skill. But he played the one year because he was challenged by a friend to prove he wasn't a coward.

Still it was baseball that he enjoyed more than any other game, and here, too, he became a standout player. He was the first baseman on the school team and developed into a power hitter. There are stories still told of Young Hank's hitting a ball so far in some city public parks that no one could find the ball.

In his senior year, in 1929, the Monroe team made the finals of the city championship. Hank would remember this day with chagrin. Not only did his team lose 4–1, and not only did Hank go hitless, but he allowed a ground ball to go through his legs for a triple, which damaged the team's chances.

"I wasn't a great ballplayer in high school," Hank said later, "but my old basketball coach, Irwin Dickstein, wasn't far off when he said, 'Hank never played games, he worked at them. He wasn't a natural athlete. His body reactions were slow, and he had trouble coordinating his big body. He couldn't run a lick because

He was the first baseman on the school team and developed into a power hitter.

10

of his flat feet. . . . I believe his size made him self-conscious. He was a great competitor because he hated to lose to smaller boys.'" Hank, however, maintained he hated to lose to anyone, regardless of size.

The coach had hit upon something that Hank would acknowledge. He threw himself into sports with such ferocity because of an inferiority complex. Hank in later years said that one reason he spent so much time trying to excel in sports was because at age thirteen he had grown so tall, he was taller than almost all of the other students. He was embarrassed to have to squeeze into the small desks in the classrooms. He was awkward and had a bad case of acne. When he went to the blackboard, he did it with great discomfort, feeling everyone was laughing at him.

Classmates giggled because Hank towered over the teacher. He was always being teased about his height. He heard many times a day: "How's the weather up there?" When friends of the family visited, they would exclaim, "My God! Look at how much he's grown! He's grown two feet in a week!"

"I was beginning to feel like a freak," Hank said later. "So sports was my escape."

Greenberg was now making quite a reputation for himself as an athlete, especially a baseball player. He played in various leagues around the city. One of them was called the Bronx Quarter League. Each player put up twenty-five cents, and the winning team won all. Yet for such a meager amount, the games were fierce. And sometimes fights would break out. It was not unusual for the game to end in the sixth or seventh inning, with the umpire having fled for his life.

In the summer of 1929, after Greenberg had graduated from high school, he continued to practice at
Crotona Park. Through the years he had developed a
difficult relationship with a man named Pat McDonald,
who practiced the shot put there, regularly thrusting
from his shoulder a heavy metal ball to see how far he
could throw it. McDonald had been on the Olympic
team for the shot-put event in 1912. He was a huge,
formidable-looking man, about six feet five, 275 pounds.
He was also a police captain, so he carried with him
even more authority. He'd often be winding up with
great fury to heave his shot, when suddenly one of
Greenberg's batted balls would bounce close to him. Or
sometimes Greenberg or one of his friends darted in
pursuit of a ball across McDonald's path. The shot put-
ter had to put on the brakes. Then he'd huff and puff
and holler. "He became like a mad bull," Hank recalled.

Hank, like his friends, never wanted to get too close
to McDonald. But one day, which happened to be the
season opener for the Yankees, McDonald came to the
field and called Hank over. Hank came, with under-
standable concern.

"Young man," said McDonald, in his Irish brogue, "I
just came from watching the Yankees play and, by God,
you hit the ball better than Lou Gehrig." Hank would
recall that was the finest compliment he had received
until that point, especially from someone who was prac-
tically a mortal enemy. It was also the first time that
Hank thought that he might have a chance to become a
professional baseball player.

Hank had never dreamed of becoming a professional. Few of them came out of New York City, other

12

than a rare exception like Lou Gehrig, the Yankees' slugging first baseman. The boys rarely went to Yankee Stadium or the Polo Grounds, the two major-league parks near Hank's house. Tickets were too expensive for their limited budgets.

Greenberg had heard that some New York kids with baseball talent were allowed to shag flies, or to run after and catch balls, in the Polo Grounds with the substitute players of the Giants. He sought permission to do so. His father asked a business acquaintance, who was one of the directors of the Giants, if his son might get an opportunity to spend a morning at the ballpark. Unknown to Hank, the Giants had already scouted him, and John McGraw, the famous, crusty manager of the team, had determined that Hank was too awkward to ever make a big-league ballplayer.

So the word came back from his father's friend: Sorry, but no.

It was a blow to Hank, but it wasn't the end. He went back to practicing hitting like never before. He would get to Crotona Park at seven or eight in the morning, before anyone else. He'd throw the ball up and crack it out. As soon as others showed up, he enlisted them into shagging the fly balls. Then he'd let them hit and he'd run after their balls.

There were more games, more leagues. Soon other scouts were looking at him, and unlike the McGraw crowd, some liked what they saw. He was asked to join a semipro league, and he played for a team in Massachusetts, where he did fairly well. One day a scout from the Washington Senators approached Greenberg. The Senators were playing the Red Sox in Boston, he said.

Would Hank like to take batting practice with his club? Like to? Was he kidding?

Shortly after, Hank found himself dressing in the Senators' clubhouse. He then moved to the dugout. It was a thrill for him to gawk at all the star players whom he had read about in the newspapers.

Hank felt awkward and self-conscious. Most of the players wouldn't even look at him. One though, a pitcher named Fred Marberry, said, "How about a catch, kid?" Marberry had felt a little sorry for the newcomer. After the catch, the Senators' manager, the former great pitcher Walter Johnson, signalled Hank to step into the batting cage.

Greenberg proceeded to either miss every pitch or foul it off. The other players began to crowd around, growling, "Get him out of there." After about twenty cuts, without Hank's having hit a fair ball, Johnson said, "Okay. That's enough, kid."

And it was, for the Senators. Now Hank was dead with them and the Giants. But others had also been watching Greenberg. One, Paul Krichell of the Yankees, was the same scout who had discovered Gehrig. He had looked Greenberg over in high school, as had Jean Dubuc of the Detroit Tigers. Both felt the young man had great potential.

Krichell, in fact, invited Hank to attend a Yankee game with him the summer after high school. They sat in first-row box seats right by the Yankee dugout. Krichell was telling Hank that Gehrig didn't have many years left and that one day soon Hank might very well be at first base for the Yankees.

About at that moment, Gehrig came out of the dug-out to get to the on-deck circle as the next batter. Greenberg took notice of him and was awed. His shoulders were wide, his legs looked powerful, and he was still pretty young.

"That Lou Gehrig looks like he's got a lot of years left," said Greenberg.

Krichell shook his head. "Look at how his batting average has slipped," he said. Slipped? thought Greenberg. The guy is still batting about .300 and still hits long home runs.

"No way I'm going to sign with this team," Greenberg said to himself.

Greenberg was right about Gehrig, who still had a number of good years left. Now Greenberg turned his attention to Dubuc of the Tigers. At this time, Greenberg, at the urging of his parents, had enrolled at New York University. Dubuc offered Greenberg three thousand dollars in cash to sign and another six thousand when he finished his freshman year in college and reported to the Tigers to play minor-league ball in their farm system.

Greenberg now had to discuss this matter with his family. This was in a period, the late 1920s, when many people still did not look upon baseball as a business and as a proper profession for young men. It was, despite its immense popularity, still known for its rowdy ballplayers, a tobacco-chewing and spitting crowd, and for a short career that left the athlete with little more than his memories.

Greenberg's parents had dreams of their son becoming a professional man, but in business or medicine or the law. They still thought he should be studying rather than playing ball.

"Pop," Hank said to his father, "are you against baseball as a career?"

He nodded.

"The Tigers offered me nine thousand dollars."

Mr. Greenberg whistled softly. "Nine thousand dollars?" he said. "You mean they want to give you that kind of money to play baseball?"

"That's right," said Hank.

"And they'll let you finish college first?"

"Yes."

Mr. Greenberg sat down to gather his thoughts. "I thought baseball was a game," he said, after a moment. "But it's a business—apparently a very good business. Take the money."

Greenberg had signed with the Tigers rather than the Yankees without knowing anything about the organization, the town, or the ballpark, Navin Field. He just knew that because of Gehrig, the Yankees weren't for him. He was aware, however, of the great tradition of baseball in Detroit, with such stars as Ty Cobb, Sam Crawford, Harry Heilman, and Hughie Jennings.

Hank began classes at NYU, but after the fall term, in January, 1930, he got the urge to play baseball. He could smell the grass and feel the contact of hitting a ball and the welcome surge through his arms. He looked eagerly toward the challenge of becoming a big-league ballplayer. He began to think more and more of spring training in Florida.

"Pop," said Hank, "I've got to go down there. I've got to play."

"What about college?" his father asked.

"College can come later," Hank replied. "Right now I want to play ball."

So Hank wrote the owner of the Tigers, Frank Navin, for permission to join the ball club. Soon he received a railroad ticket to Tampa, Florida, where the team trained. Hank Greenberg, now nineteen, with a baseball glove in his cloth suitcase, boarded a train in bustling Penn Station and headed for a new world.

2

Struggle in the Minors

None of the other Tiger players mingled with the raw rookie named Hank Greenberg. They had little to do with him either in the clubhouse, or on the field, or at the team's hotel. It was simply the way veterans treated rookies in general, though it came as little comfort to the young recruit that he wasn't alone in his misery.

When he first arrived in Tampa in March of 1930, Hank sat around the Tigers clubhouse in his white flannel baseball uniform, blue-scripted *Detroit* across his chest, wearing his white-and-blue Tiger cap, with his eyes wide and his mouth shut. He looked at such famous Tiger players as Dale Alexander, Harry Rice, Roy Johnson, Bob "Fat" Fothergill, and two future Hall-of-Famers, the pitcher Waite Hoyt and the second baseman Charlie Gehringer.

They were all grown men, well-groomed and well-dressed when they wore street clothes. Most had been in the major leagues for quite a few years.

"I guess most of them didn't understand why I was there," Hank recalled. "I was an eager beaver and chased a lot of balls and did a lot of shagging, and occasionally they let me take batting practice. I could hit a long ball, even though these weren't game conditions, and the pitching was a lot easier."

The only person whom Hank became friendly with in Tampa was a clubhouse boy, Alex Okray, who would later become a clubhouse boy for the Tigers in Detroit. Alex was about the same age as Hank, and this was also his first year away from home.

"Don't worry about the snubs, Hank," Okray said. "It's just part of the game." He explained that these veterans had seen Hank as a threat to take their jobs, or their friends' jobs, and none of them took kindly to it.

After dinner at the hotel, the players would sit out on the lawn near a bandstand and listen to the music. It was at these times that Hank would tell Alex about his dreams of breaking into the lineup of the Tigers. And it looked, from Hank's performance in training camp, that it might not be very far off.

One day in batting practice Hank lined a pitch back to the mound that sent the pitcher, Lefty Page, to the doctor. A few minutes later, another pitcher was sent sprawling by a smash off Hank's bat. Some of the regulars grumbled that Hank was trying to destroy the pitching staff.

Before an exhibition game soon thereafter, Bucky Harris, the Tiger manager, came up to Greenberg. "Hank," he said, "you're starting today."

The Tigers were playing the Boston Braves. Green-

Hank Greenberg with Charlie Gehringer

berg was about to play in his first game with a major-league team. He was understandably nervous. Just before the game, the Braves' starting pitcher, Johnny Cooney, took Hank aside. "Kid," he said, "I'm gonna give you one you can hit." Hank didn't know why Cooney would help him, though he surmised that perhaps he had heard of Hank's problems with the older players on the club.

Cooney kept his word and threw Hank a fat pitch, which the youngster walloped over the fence for a home run.

The next morning, one of the Detroit newspapers reported: "Henry Greenberg, the prize rookie, stole the show. He made a couple of sensational plays at first base. His first chance was right in the dirt and he dug it up, and his trip to the plate resulted in a home run and Babe Ruth never hit a ball harder." The article went on to say that Hank was "the greatest prospect in years," and that it was "a joke on Col. Jake Ruppert, owner of the Yankees. Greenberg lives only two blocks from Yankee Stadium."

It was laudatory, of course, and a little exaggerated, including the reference to Greenberg's home, which was several miles from Yankee Stadium. But it foreshadowed things to come.

However, as Hank discovered, there were not many people like Johnny Cooney. Soon he was getting his share of strikeouts and pop outs. By the end of spring training, Hank learned that he was being farmed out to Hartford, of the Class A Eastern League.

Lou Gehrig had once played for Hartford, and had been a star. Some thought Hank was the second coming of Gehrig, and expectations were high. Too high. Greenberg, being young and so inexperienced in this his first professional year, felt the pressure and couldn't live up to it. He tried hard but felt, around first base, "as big and awkward as a giraffe." He missed pop flies over his head, and his feet got tangled up on ground balls. He also struck out thirteen straight times.

After twelve games he was batting just .214. "I'm a total bust," he told himself. Even though he hit a home run and a triple in his last game, the Tigers decided to send him to a lower level of competition with the Raleigh, North Carolina, team in the Class C Piedmont League.

Hank was dragging, perhaps feeling sorry for himself, and wondering if he had made a mistake in trying to become a baseball player. He joined Raleigh and before he knew it, he was playing poorly there, too. Things had gone from bad to terrible.

He felt he didn't fit in. He was still ungainly for one thing, and the setting was strange, too. He was a kid from a big city who had been thrown in with a bunch of farm boys. Before one game, Hank was standing in the outfield when he became aware of a teammate walking slowly around him and staring.

"What're you looking at?" asked Greenberg.

"Nothing," the player said. "I've never seen a Jew before. I'm just looking."

Hank felt as though he were an animal in a zoo. "See anything interesting?" he asked.

"I don't understand it," he said. "You look just like anybody else."

"Thanks," said Greenberg.

Greenberg thought perhaps the player had expected to see somebody in a yarmulke and a long beard, or, as Greenberg recalled, "someone with horns." Hank encountered some nasty remarks from fans and some opposing players about being a Jew, but there was much more curiosity, like that of his teammate.

None of this helped his hitting, either. But one day, something did. The team was making a road trip. One of Hank's teammates, a pitcher named Dusty, hollered the full length of the bus to Greenberg. "Look at you, you big bum!" he shouted. "What a slugger you are! I'm hitting .155 and you're slugging along at a terrific pace of .151!"

Greenberg would always remember that, and how angry it made him. In some ways, he would see it as a turning point in his career. That day, Hank got four hits in four times at bat. He soon lifted his batting average to around .300, and finished the year at .314. He had hit 19 home runs and batted in 93 runs and was one of the team's leaders in both those departments.

As he began to adjust to the team, and to life in the South, another event, one that he called significant, took place. He went on his first date with a girl. In high school, perhaps because of his self-consciousness and his interest in sports, he had had no time for girls. Some of his friends had, and they dragged him along to talk to girls, but it went no further than that. But in Raleigh one day, he was approached by a fan who introduced himself.

The man was Jewish and invited Hank to his home

for the traditional Friday night dinner. Hank accepted eagerly. When he arrived, he met the man's wife and their daughter. After dinner, the parents left Hank and their daughter alone. Hank, feeling stuck, asked her to a movie. They went, and afterward he took her for a soda and then home. Not only was this his first date with a girl, it was his last date with that girl. There were no sparks.

Meanwhile, Hank was going about his business of being a baseball player. He went to the ballpark on his days off and practiced, and on game days he got there early and practiced. He was now getting to be a valued and well-liked member of the team. And so it wasn't difficult to persuade several of them to come out and

Hank was becoming a valued member of the team.

practice with him. In small towns, there wasn't much else to do.

The bus rides in the minor leagues are legendary, and Hank never forgot his, either. The team traveled from one end of North Carolina to the next on an old and decrepit bus. When it groaned up a hill at about two miles an hour, the players would be yelling, "Giddyap, bus, giddyap!"

One of Hank's best friends on the team was a small, thin infielder called Flea Clifton. Flea was a good player and had some unusual characteristics. He soaked his bat in water because that was supposed to keep it from cracking. And on the road he would eat nothing but doughnuts and bananas. He said that they were filling and stretched the meal money. Hank joked with Flea that he was the only person who could show a profit on a-dollar-a-day allowance.

Toward the end of his first season in Raleigh, Hank had impressed the Tigers organization so much that they called him to Detroit to travel with the club for the last three weeks of the 1930 major-league season. The Tigers were in fifth place out of eight teams in the American League, and well behind the Philadelphia A's, who went on to win the pennant easily. So Hank thought he'd get a good deal of playing time to show the team officials what he could do.

For about the first week, though, about all he did was run after balls in batting practice and take his swings in the batting cage. He couldn't even get to practice at first base, because there always seemed someone on there, particularly Earl Whitehill, the star pitcher who also fancied himself an ace first baseman. And the reaction of the players to Hank was generally about the same as it had been during spring training. It was as if he didn't exist. During games, he sat by himself on the bench.

In one game against the Yankees, the Tigers fell hopelessly behind and were unable to hit the Yankee pitching star, Red Ruffing. Suddenly Hank heard his name called by the manager, Bucky Harris. "Get a bat," said Harris. Greenberg went up to pinch hit. It was his first official at bat in the big leagues and, as he recalled, he was "scared to death."

As he kneeled in the on-deck circle, he looked out on the field and saw such players as Ruth and Gehrig and Bill Dickey, the great catcher, and Tony Lazzeri, the star second baseman. "What am I doing here?" he asked himself.

He was so frightened that he was as good as out even before stepping into the batter's box. "I don't know how I got up to the plate," he recalled, "or what I swung at, or how I even connected with the ball." He popped up to Lazzeri.

But this broke the ice. He knew that the next time he batted, he would really be ready. He'd show the Tigers just what he could do.

One game passed without him playing, and another, and another. Hank sat and sat and sat. He couldn't understand why he wasn't given a chance. The regular first baseman, Dale Alexander, was one of the best hitters on the team. But since the team was out of the pennant race, Hank wondered why wouldn't they let him play first base, even a little.

At this time, Jean Dubuc, who had signed Hank to a Tiger contract, was a coach in uniform with the team. Hank kept asking him when he'd get a chance.

"Don't worry, Hank," Dubuc said. "You'll get in again."

Then it was the last day of the season. Hank packed up his Model A Ford, the car he had bought in Raleigh for $350 and which he regularly polished with loving care, and drove to Navin Field for the game.

Hank was in a chipper mood. Surely, he thought, he'd play in this game, possibly even start. It was a totally unimportant game in the standings. When he checked the lineup card that had been posted on the clubhouse door, he saw that Dale Alexander was penciled in at first base.

Well, thought Hank, maybe Dale will take one turn at bat, and then I'll go in.

Alexander batted once, he batted twice, he batted a third time. The game wound down to the eighth inning. Hank was sitting at the end of the bench and fuming. Even if he got in now, he might not even get a chance to bat. And just then, Harris yelled, "Greenberg, get in there and play first base."

By now, Hank was beside himself with anger. He stood up, bumped his head on the dugout roof, and said to the manager, "I ain't gonna play for this team."

Then he stormed past the rest of the shocked players, down the runway and into the clubhouse. He swiftly changed into his street clothes, hurried out of the clubhouse, and jumped into his car. He headed east, for home, boiling mad.

When he finally arrived in New York, Hank's luck

hadn't changed much. He ran a red light. A large Irish policeman stopped him and motioned him to pull over to the curb. The policeman looked over the car. Then he asked for Hank's license and looked that over, too. The car still had North Carolina license plates.

"What do you do for a living?" the policeman asked.

"I'm a professional baseball player," Hank replied.

The policeman looked back at the license plate and began laughing. Hank had no idea what was so funny.

"And who ever heard of a professional baseball player named Greenberg?" the policeman said, still chuckling.

After all, there were very few Jewish players in the big leagues, then or before, while the rosters were filled with Irish players. But to Hank, that incident was a fitting end to his exasperating experience of the last three weeks.

At home, Hank saw that he had become a kind of celebrity. Friends and family came to the Greenberg household to see Hank and to talk about the summer. It was as though Hank had grown up, suddenly, and become a man of the world. Bold enough, in fact, to write Frank Navin, the owner of the Tigers, and give him his thoughts on his past, present, and future.

Hank told Navin that he was unhappy with his treatment in Detroit and also with his being assigned to Beaumont of the Texas League, a Class AA team. Hank had developed a good bit of confidence from his season with Raleigh and decided that he should move up faster.

Navin wrote back, and with firmness, beginning the letter with, not "Dear Hank," but "Dear Mr. Greenberg."

"Baseball is not run for the youngster," Navin wrote. "Relative to the bad treatment you received in Detroit, we took you to Detroit so you could get acquainted with major league surroundings and not to play ball, thinking it might help you. If it had come about that Manager Harris could have used you in a game he would undoubtedly have done so. It seems to me it comes with rather poor grace from a boy who has just made good in Class C to criticize a Manager of Harris's well-known ability. . . .

"Of course, it may be possible that a younger and brighter school of ballplayers is developing, who know more than the manager and coaches of a major league club, but at this time I will have to string along with the players who have demonstrated their ability on the field.

"So far as I am concerned, if you do not see fit to accept the contract tendered you by the Beaumont Club, that is a matter entirely up to you.

"Very truly yours,
Frank J. Navin."

Greenberg read over the letter. He still didn't think he was wrong about his Detroit experience, nor about believing that he could do better than the Class AA Beaumont club, which, in fact, was the Tigers' top farm team. But Greenberg was also not about to end his relationship with the Tigers. For one thing, he liked the organization over all. Where else might have he had a chance to be on a big-league team even for three weeks, at age nineteen? For another thing, he still would be getting the rest of his six thousand dollars for having signed with them.

So, after a pleasant winter's rest in New York, and having stayed in shape by regularly playing handball and basketball, he again packed up his Model A. It took Hank four and a half days to make the trip from the Bronx to training camp in Orange, Texas, about thirty miles from Beaumont. When he pulled into town, he saw men walking around with guns and holsters.

The team, meanwhile, stayed in a boardinghouse for seven dollars a week plus three huge meals daily. His closet was the shower.

He wasn't there long enough to get comfortable, or uncomfortable, either. Beaumont had a first baseman named Ray Fritz, who had played with Evansville, the Tigers' Class B team, the year before. He was set to be Beaumont's first baseman for the coming 1931 season. Very quickly, as Fritz was sent up a notch, Hank Greenberg was sent down. He was assigned to Evansville of the Three-I League (the I's were Illinois, Indiana, and Iowa). Though a step up from Raleigh, it was a long way from Detroit.

Hank knew why Fritz was moving up, but he also questioned the commitment the Tigers had for him. Hank wondered: Had his letter to Navin made the club sour on him a little?

"Going down to Evansville was a big disappointment to me," Greenberg recalled. "But I went."

He was twenty years old, and he truly thought, This is my last chance.

3

A Detroit Tiger

Bouncing along at night on the Evansville team bus, Hank and a few of the other young, hopeful ballplayers sometimes actually sat on the roof with the baggage. In the warm night breeze, and as the dark, flat lands of the Midwest and the lights in the farmhouses rolled by, they often passed the time singing some of the old-time songs, such as "Let Me Call You Sweetheart" and "Sidewalks of New York."

In Evansville, Hank lived in a boardinghouse with a family, the Tonnemachers, that he grew close to. And he continued to apply himself to baseball with his customary diligence. Because of his concern for his future, he "dug in," as he phrased it. Years later, he recalled this period as one of the happiest of his life.

It was particularly happy because he was succeeding

The ballplayers often sat on the roof of the bus.

at baseball. He wound up the regular season for Evansville with a .318 batting average, including 15 home runs, and leading the league in doubles, with 41. But he still made mistakes, particularly in the field, and so also led the league in errors at first base, with 25. Evansville made the league playoffs. They were playing for the division title in Quincy, Illinois, when on one play, Hank slid hard into third base. Cap Crosley, the Quincy third baseman, tagged him hard, and the two got into a squabble. The hometown fans began to shout and curse at Greenberg.

After the game his teammates rushed him into the dugout as the fans swarmed the field, snarling and calling him names. "It was scary," Hank recalled. There was no police protection in those ballparks, and the Evansville players had to form a cordon around Hank to get him to the team bus. Headlines in the following day's paper told of how Greenberg was "barely saved."

There was more fan abuse for Greenberg in the game the following day, but, as luck would have it, Quincy won, and Hank got out of there in one piece.

His performance for Evansville, meanwhile, was good enough to merit him a promotion, back to the Beaumont Exporters of the Texas League for the 1932 season.

"Beaumont," Hank said, "was hot as blazes, and we only played day games there. To make matters worse, someone came up with the idea of having red uniforms. So we sweated in these heavy, coarse horse blankets for uniforms while playing in temperatures of a hundred degrees."

They played night games in Galveston and Houston where they could see the heat come shimmering off the field in waves. Saltwater mosquitoes attacked them like dive bombers. Visiting teams didn't have showers. The players had to return to their hotels where they hung up their wet uniforms on slow-turning ceiling fans. Their cramped rooms smelled like gymnasiums.

Because some of the cities in the Texas League were so far apart—as much as 400 miles—the teams took trains instead of buses. There was no air-conditioning on the trains, so in order to have some air to breathe, the players had to open the windows. When they did, cinders would blow in, covering them with soot. One player would yell, "Open those windows!" And another would holler, "Close those windows!"

Taking a train even some of the time—as opposed to

bus travel in most minor leagues all of the time—was just one step closer to the major leagues. In the major leagues, of course, all of the teams traveled by train all of the time.

The season with Beaumont was a giant step toward that goal for Hank. He led the league with 39 home runs and batted in 131 runs. Beaumont won the Texas League championship, and Hank was voted the Most Valuable Player in the league. On the strength of his good year at Beaumont, he was invited to the Tigers training camp the following spring.

It was wonderful, and it was embarrassing. For the first time Hank would be seeing some of the players who had watched him in what he called "my great moment of shame." That was on the last day of the 1930 season when he had gotten mad at Bucky Harris in the Tiger dugout and rushed to the clubhouse in tears, bawling that he would never play for the Tigers.

But no one seemed to hold it against him, or even remind him of it. What he did find unpleasant was that Bucky Harris handed him a fielder's glove and told him to try third base. The Tigers had just bought Harry Davis, a fancy-fielding first baseman with no power, for $75,000, on Harris's recommendation. Davis had had a decent year in 1932, hitting .270.

Greenberg, meanwhile, had never played anywhere but first base and was surprised and disappointed by this move. But he worked hard trying to learn third base. The result was captured by a Detroit sportswriter, who wrote that Greenberg was "a big sweaty kid who looked pretty grotesque. . . ." He added that Hank was too big, that he wouldn't be able to stand the major-league pace, that he would get fat and slow down, and would suffer from fallen arches: "Big fellows like that always get fallen arches."

He criticized Greenberg the fielder as being too clumsy and Greenberg the hitter as being too much of a free swinger.

Fortunately, not everyone agreed with that assessment. One of those was Hank Greenberg, though he eagerly sought to end the third-base experiment. Eventually he got his wish, and Hank returned to playing first base. He regularly stayed very late at practice, having a coach hit him ground ball after ground ball.

"How long are you gonna keep that coach out there hitting fungoes?" asked a newspaperman.

"Till I can field first base as well as Harry Davis," said Hank.

"That'll be a long time," said the newspaperman.

Hank was hitting the ball hard in batting practice and in exhibition games. And when the 1933 season began, he was wearing a Tiger uniform. But that was all. After the first several games of the season, he was doing little more than sitting and watching.

He complained to the manager. He complained to the coaches. Nothing. One day he went up to Frank Navin's office to speak with the owner.

"I can't play ball sitting on the bench," Hank blurted out. "If you people don't want me to play, then let me go someplace where I can."

"You'll get your chance to play," said Navin. "I promise you."

Two weeks later, apparently after a phone call from Navin, Bucky Harris scratched out Harry Davis's name on the lineup card, and wrote in "Greenberg."

In that game, against St. Louis, Greenberg went hitless in three at-bats. He sat on the bench again for three more weeks.

Then he got another chance, made a few hits, and began to appear in the lineup more frequently. He hit his first major-league home run on May 6. Soon he was the regular first baseman, and Harry Davis was relegated to Hank's old spot on the dugout bench.

Of all the ballparks around the league, Hank liked his home park, Navin Field, best. It was a relatively small ballpark, with the intimacy of stands close to the playing field. Sometimes it seemed that the fans were actually hovering over the foul lines. Navin Field also had a left-field fence which, for most of his career there, was about 340 feet down the line. A good distance, but not a killer distance—not, say, like Yankee Stadium, which, though just 301 feet directly down the line, quickly shot back to 460 feet in left-center field.

Hank was soon so comfortable with his surroundings in his rookie year that he even got thrown out of a game, one of the few times this happened in his entire career.

The plate umpire, George Moriarty, had called strike three on Greenberg on a pitch that he and the Tiger manager, Bucky Harris, considered wide. Harris ran out of the dugout and protested vigorously. Moriarty seemed hardly to listen to the Harris tirade. Then Harris, growing tired of this, turned and started back to the dugout. But Hank, who had been silent, said, "That goes for me, too."

Moriarty wheeled, and shouted: "Get out of here, you fresh busher! You're out of the game!" Greenberg learned a lesson. A veteran can argue; a rookie has to gradually earn his right to dispute an umpire.

Hank was also learning about being a major leaguer on other levels. This was the middle of the Depression, and money and jobs were terribly scarce. People waited in long lines, for example, to get a bowl of soup. It was said that even brain surgeons sold apples on street corners, and that was not far from the truth.

Hank and the ballplayers would follow a routine after breakfast in their hotel. They'd sit in the lobby and wait until it was time to go to the ballpark. They'd want to read the newspapers, but they'd wait until some other guest would finish with his paper. As soon as he laid it on the chair, several of the players would make a mad dash to get it. In those days, a newspaper cost two cents. The players laughed about it, but none of them wanted to spend the money. Going to the park, four or five of the players would crowd into one taxi in order to split the fare.

Something else Hank was learning: There was a great deal of bench jockeying, or razzing by opponents, in the league. Greenberg was one of the biggest targets.

"Greenberg," wrote a Detroit newspaperman, "was a little different from anybody else on the team. In a sense he was different from anybody else in the league. He was the only Jewish ballplayer around and presented no problem away from the field." [Actually,

The Yankees had a couple of expert bench jockeys.

there were a handful of Jewish players in the major leagues, such as Moe Berg, Harry Danning, Milton Galatzer, Phil Weintraub, and Buddy Myer, who was half Jewish, but none would ever be as prominent as Greenberg.] "At the ballpark," added the writer, "it was different. They would shout slurs at him, particularly the Yankees."

The Yankees had a couple of players who were their expert bench jockeys. And while they called the German players "Krauts," the Irish players "Micks," the Italians "Wops," and the Polish players "Dumb Polaks," Greenberg felt that they had reserved "a little extra for me," since he was the lone Jewish player really making a name for himself. They called him "Kike," "Sheenie," and "Jew Bastard."

For his entire career, Greenberg would hear something like this every day, in every game. On some days, he heard it at every time at bat. And he heard it not just from opposing players, but from fans, too.

Oddly enough, Greenberg said that though it made him mad, it also made him try harder. "I wanted to show them what I could do," he explained. In fact, after that very first home run Hank hit in the major leagues, against the Senators in Detroit, a reporter noted that Greenberg had turned "razzberries" into "a deafening and prolonged cheer as he crossed the plate."

In the earlier years of baseball, some Jewish players even changed their names to make life less difficult. There were, for example, a pitcher named Kane and infielders named Bohne, Cooney, and Ewing. Each of them was born Cohen. There was also a second baseman for the Giants in the 1920s named Cohen who kept his name: Andy Cohen. He came with a great deal of fanfare from the press, but he never quite lived up to expectations. Perahaps the best-acknowledged Jewish player before Greenberg was Erskine Mayer, a pitcher for the Philadelphia Phillies who won twenty-one games in both 1914 and 1915.

But Greenberg couldn't concern himself very much with history. He felt that he had a job to do, and a place to do it in. He liked the town of Detroit and quickly made friends, particularly with people in the Jewish community, who were taking great pride in Hank. They wanted to give him a banquet and present him with a Cadillac. He turned it down. Other rookies weren't getting banquets just because they were in the major leagues, and he didn't want to be treated so obviously differently. He also was being asked to dine out with families nearly every night. But he generally refused the invitations. He felt he'd better keep his mind on baseball and his waistline in playing trim. He thought that that kind of attention, as well-meaning as it was, helped destroy Andy Cohen.

Nonetheless, Greenberg also felt an obligation and responsibility to his fellow Jews. He had always understood that he was important to them as a symbol and a beacon, even though he felt that there sometimes was too much pressure exerted on him. After all, it was hard enough trying to hit a major-league fastball without also having to carry the hopes and dreams of an entire people. Yet Greenberg did, and he made sure there was never a scandal associated with his name.

"I always tried to live within the proper bounds of

my religion," he once said, "and have never done anything to bring discredit on Jews."

Hank finished the 1933 season with a very respectable .301 batting average, 12 home runs, and 87 runs batted in. He was earning $600 a month, or $3,300 for a five-and-a-half-month season as a major-league player. He had also established himself as the Tigers' regular first baseman, and this was a wonderful and glamorous position for a young man in America. There was something else, too. Hank now had a steady job, which was no small thing during the Depression.

And now when he returned home, he was no longer a semicelebrity. He was a full-blown one. Family, and even friends and neighbors, were asked to pose for newspaper photographs. "Look at you," Hank's mother said to him, "the Napoleon of the Bronx!"

He had loved that first year in the major leagues and had been able to play against Babe Ruth, who he would say was the greatest player he'd ever seen. The Babe was by then pretty hefty, but he could still wallop those long home runs and still amaze in the field. One day, with the Babe in left field, a Tiger player hit a long drive. Ruth turned to the stands as though to watch the ball go over his head, then he suddenly turned back to the field, caught the ball, and threw out the unsuspecting runner at second base. "What timing!" Hank exclaimed. "I never saw anything like that before!"

As for Hank's own situation, he was again writing Navin. This time he was asking for more money. His previous contract called for him to earn a monthly salary. This meant that if the parent club sent him back to the minor leagues, it could also reduce his salary. But if he got a major-league contract, they couldn't. He also felt he was entitled to at least $1,000 a month, or $5,500 a year, a $2,200 raise.

"You had a good year for a youngster," Navin wrote, "and there is no reason why you cannot go on, although it will be more difficult for you this year because the pitchers will pay more attention to you and work on your weaknesses more than last year."

He said he'd give Hank a raise to $4,500. Hank stood his ground, though he was nervous. Finally, after much haggling, Navin said, "Okay, five thousand dollars, plus a five hundred dollar bonus if the team ends up either one, two, three in the standings." Hank thought this was ridiculous because the Tigers hadn't finished higher than fourth in nine years.

"Mr. Navin," said Greenberg, "thank you very much. I'll be there for spring training on March first, sir."

4

"Jew Bastard!"

Among the palm trees in Lakeland, Florida, in the spring of 1934, the Tigers looked promising. They had some good young players, like left-handed pitching ace Schoolboy Rowe, outfielder Pete Fox, second baseman Gehringer, and, of course, the second-year first baseman, Greenberg. And they had also added by way of trades some new players with solid big-league credentials, like outfielder Leon ("Goose") Goslin and pitchers Alvin ("General") Crowder and Fred ("Firpo") Marberry. It was Marberry who, as a Washington Senator, had befriended Greenberg by playing catch with him in Hank's brief tryout in Fenway Park five years earlier.

But the most important addition to the Tigers was the new manager and catcher, Mickey Cochrane. A tough competitor, Cochrane, known as Black Mike for his no-nonsense attitude, had been the catcher the three times the Philadelphia A's won the pennant: in 1929, 1930 and 1931. And it was Cochrane, in Greenberg's estimation, who would teach the Tigers to win, by giving them a stirring example to follow. "He would go through a wall to catch a ball," said Greenberg.

There was also a rookie pitcher in camp from Alabama named Truett ("Rip") Sewell. He had pitched in five games for the Tigers without a decision in 1932, returned to the minor leagues, and now was trying to get back to the Tigers. After an exhibition game with the Cardinals in St. Petersburg, the Tigers were taking the bus back to Lakeland. Sitting two seats behind Greenberg was Sewell. The Tigers had lost, and Hank had not had a good day, going for the collar, as the ballplayers say; that is, getting no hits.

Sewell began needling Hank. Then he began throwing little pieces of folded-up paper. He made more remarks and laughed.

"Please cut it out, Rip," said Greenberg.

"I'm not doing anything," said Sewell.

"Yes, you are," said Greenberg. "Now leave me alone."

"Aw, what the hell's wrong with you?"

"Listen, Rip," said Greenberg, "when this bus reaches Lakeland and we get off, I'm going to beat the hell out of you. I just want you to think about it from here until we get back there." Everybody laughed.

One man didn't. It was the shortstop, Billy Rogell. He would recall that Sewell had said something like "You Jew bastard."

When the bus finally stopped in Lakeland, the team

Greenberg grabbed Sewell. "Now leave me alone," Hank said.

got off, and Greenberg was waiting for Sewell. There was a fight. Hank punched him several times; Sewell dived to try to tackle Greenberg. It was soon broken up.

When Cochrane asked Greenberg what happened, Hank told him. Then Cochrane spoke with Sewell. Not long afterward, Cochrane sent Sewell back to the minor leagues.

Greenberg was sensitive to words, but he tried not to let them influence his approach in a negative way. In fact, he said he tried to convince himself that, with men on base and everybody calling him names, they were really afraid of him and that he had the edge. He was also the only player to swing three bats in the on-deck circle. Others swung only two. As he stepped to the plate, he tossed two bats aside, dug in in the batter's box, and glared at the pitcher, as if to say, "Come on and throw it. I'll knock it downtown."

Whether this tactic indeed struck fear into the hearts of pitchers is debatable. What it did for certain, however, was build up Hank's confidence. That was the important thing.

He also studied the game thoroughly, keeping a book on the pitchers: what they liked to throw and in what situations. A curve ball after a first strike? Did the pitcher try to keep it low? On the outside corner?

Greenberg, wrote a Detroit reporter, "is the most energetic researcher in baseball . . . and is tireless in his quest for perfection, wants to know all the answers and isn't backward about asking.

"He argues continually with anyone at any time, probing calmly into other people's minds for information, knowledge, and ideas. He has a mind of his own, too, a good one, which he exercises as religiously as he does his muscles.

"He parrots no opinions, but challenges any statement which is not in line with his experience. He does it not to be contentious or contrary, but to find the answers.

"This active, inquiring turn of mind is a large factor in Greenberg's improvement."

And he continued to practice and practice. He still came early to the ballpark for batting practice, sometimes enlisting vendors and groundskeepers along with some of the young players to pitch to him and shag fly balls. One day the team was playing at Shibe Park in Philadelphia. The head groundskeeper refused to let him on the field. Greenberg argued, but to no avail. No one had noticed an elderly gentleman sitting in the stands alone. He called to Greenberg.

"I very much admire what you're doing," the man said. "You tell that groundskeeper to assist you in every way possible. Tell him that those are John Shibe's instructions." The groundskeeper found no problem now in going along with the wishes of the man who owned the park.

It was turning out to be an extraordinary season for the Tigers, and for Greenberg. He moved from sixth in the batting order to cleanup hitter, batting fourth. He had started slowly in the season, but now he was hitting for power and average and driving in runs. And the Tigers had jumped into first place and were battling the Yankees for the American League championship.

Jews all across the country began to follow the Tigers and the exploits of Hank Greenberg. There were many prominent Jews in public life, such as Supreme Court Justices Benjamin Cardozo and Louis Brandeis, financier Bernard Baruch, and entertainers like Al Jolson, Edward G. Robinson, and the Marx Brothers. However, nobody was getting the headlines now like the twenty-three-year-old Hank Greenberg.

Jews had loved baseball no less than anyone else. From the time they began following it, which was from the time they came off the boats as immigrants, it represented to them, in many ways, what America was about. This was the national game. This was the common ground where you can mingle and talk with your fellow countryman, regardless of race or religion or national background. Jews had hoped for a standout Jewish player—or, as a weekly newspaper, the *American Hebrew,* termed it, "the elusive Jewish star."

Now, it seemed, they had one: Hank Greenberg. An Indianapolis Jewish newspaper had a story on Hank that was titled "The Jewish Babe Ruth." Not quite. Hank was still young and in only his second year in the big leagues. But he was making an impact.

This was also the first time in twenty-five years, or since Ty Cobb was the star of the team, that the Tigers had a chance for the pennant. And as the second week in September drew closer, Hank had a big decision to make. He had to decide if he should play on Rosh Hashanah, the Jewish New Year.

The holiday would fall on September 10, right in the middle of the pennant race, with the Red Sox in town. It is traditional for Jews to celebrate this day solemnly. But didn't Greenberg have to meet other responsibilities as well?

"We're only four games ahead of the Yankees," Greenberg told a reporter a day before the game. "Suppose I stay out and we lose the pennant by one game? That will keep the boys out of the World Series after they have worked so hard all season to get into the Series. Would that be justice? What'll they think? And what will Detroit think?"

"I didn't know what Rosh Hashanah was," recalled Eldon Auker, who was scheduled to pitch that game. All he knew was that "Hank was pretty important to us."

Some newspapermen had gone to the top rabbi in Detroit and asked if it was socially acceptable for Hank

One of Detroit's newspapers wished Greenberg a Happy New Year.

49

to play. The rabbi studied the problem. He then determined that since this was the start of a new year, it was a happy occasion, and found that Jews in the past had indeed played games on that day. So he gave Hank the okay.

On the front page of one of Detroit's daily newspapers that morning, there was a headline in Yiddish with a photograph of Hank Greenberg. Under the Yiddish was the English translation: "Happy New Year, Hank."

The game that day was close. The Red Sox scored and then Hank hit a home run in the seventh inning to tie it. Now it was the bottom of the ninth, the score still tied, 1–1. Hank again was at the plate. Gordon Rhodes threw a fast ball, and Hank swung.

"Hank met the pitch perfectly," wrote Bud Shaver. "The ball sailed on a line, the ball cleared the wall beyond the scoreboard, and Henry trotted around the bases as the crowd swarmed onto the field. At the plate, Hank was met by a milling throng and it was with difficulty that he made his way to the clubhouse." Final score: Tigers 2, Red Sox 1. Hank would remember that moment as one of the most exciting of his career.

But ten days later, there was another problem similar to this last one. It was Yom Kippur, the holiest day of the Jewish year. For Hank, the question rose again: To play or not to play.

"We are an orthodox family," David Greenberg, Hank's father, told a reporter. "Hank promised me he would not play on Rosh Hashanah or Yom Kippur. He wrote us and said he was sorry but that Mickey

Cochrane said he was needed. But," said Mr. Green-berg, "Yom Kippur is different. I put my foot my down."

Hank didn't play on Yom Kippur. It was headline news all across the nation. Edgar A. Guest, a popular syndicated poet, wrote a poem that appeared that day entitled, "Speaking of Greenberg." He wrote that the Irish didn't like it when they first heard of Greenberg's name, but they began to respect him as he displayed his hitting prowess. The poem ended like this:

Came Yom Kippur—holy fast day world wide over to the
    Jew—
And Hank Greenberg to his teaching and the old tradition
    true
Spent the day among his people and he didn't come to
    play.
Said Murphy to Mulroony, "We shall lose the game today.
We shall miss him on the infield and shall miss him at
    the bat.
But he's true to his religion—and I honor him for that."

"I was a hero around town," recalled Hank, "par-ticularly among the Jewish people, and I was very proud of that."

On Yom Kippur morning, with friends, Hank went to synagogue. He walked in while the rabbi was con-ducting services. Suddenly people began to applaud, even in synagogue. The rabbi, who had no idea what was going on, looked up. There was a tremendous ova-tion. Hank was embarrassed; he didn't know what to do. So he said, "Thank you," and took his seat in the congregation. The rabbi smiled and then went back to his prayers.

There had never been a Yom Kippur in Detroit quite like this Yom Kippur.

The Tigers won the American League pennant by seven games over the Yankees, and Hank was outstanding. He played in 153 games—missing only the game on Yom Kippur—hitting .339, with 26 homers and 139 runs batted in, third in the league in that department. He also led the league in doubles with 63.

The Tigers met the Cardinals in the World Series. The Cardinals were hot, having won 20 of their last 25 games in a tight pennant race in the National League. They were called the "Gashouse Gang" for their spirited, rough-and-tumble play. They had Frankie Frisch, the manager and second baseman, Leo Durocher at shortstop, Pepper Martin at third, and Joe Medwick in left. The stars of the pitching corps were the Dean brothers, Dizzy and Paul, who was sometimes referred to as "Daffy."

Dizzy and Daffy, despite their nicknames, weren't clowns on the mound, however. The first had won 30 games that year and the other, 19.

In the first game, in Detroit, Greenberg singled in the sixth and hit a towering home run in the eighth, but it wasn't enough, as Dizzy Dean pitched St. Louis to an 8–3 win. It would be Hank's best game.

He was having problems. He admitted before the Series that he was so nervous he could hardly eat. Beyond that, the Cardinals had some pretty good pitchers. Hank struck out four times in important situations with men on base.

And Dean needled Greenberg. "Hello, Mose," he said, using the shortened version of Moses, a rather common usage when referring to Jewish players. "What makes you so white? Boy, you're shakin' like a leaf. Ol' Diz is goin' to pitch, and he's gonna pin your ears back."

This was a personal slur at Greenberg; it was Dean's technique to rile the opposition with down-home Ozarks humor.

It worked on Hank. He swung at balls eye high that he should never have swung at, he was so anxious to knock the ball down Dizzy's throat. "Dean," Hank said afterward, "made me look like a monkey. They tell me I swung at pitches two feet over my head. I don't doubt it."

The Cardinals won the Series in seven games, the Dean brothers winning two games each. And though Hank didn't play great, he still had some moments. In fact, he ended up with 9 hits in 28 times at bat, for a .321 average. And though he hit just one homer, he did drive in 7 runs, the highest total of either team, and one short of the record for RBIs in a World Series.

Despite the overall great season, things wouldn't be normal if he didn't have a contract hassle with Navin. Neither looked forward to it, but both expected it. They met when Navin came to New York on other business.

In Navin's hotel room, Hank said that he now wanted fifteen thousand dollars for the coming year.

Navin hesitated. "Okay," he said. "I'll give you ten thousand dollars plus a five thousand dollar bonus."

"I don't care how you give it to me," said Hank, "as long as we both understand that I'll be getting fifteen thousand."

"Understood," said Navin.

Then Navin wrote out a check for five thousand dollars. Hank took it and put it in his pocket. He was afraid to take the subway back to the Bronx with so much money, so he went directly from the hotel to the Bowery Savings Bank and immediately opened an account for five thousand dollars.

Then, with a new bankbook in his pocket, and a whistle on his lips, Hank disappeared down the subway entrance.

5

Pursuit
of the Babe

In the 1935 baseball season, Hank Greenberg established himself as one of the stars of the game.

He batted .328, second on his team to Gehringer, at .330. Hank tied Jimmy Foxx for the league home-run championship with 36, and led the league with 170 runs batted in. He won the RBI title by a huge margin; the next closest was Gehrig with 119, followed by Foxx with 115. The Tigers repeated as the American League champions, again beating out the Yankees.

This time, they played the Cubs in the World Series. The Cubs were a strong veteran team, so tough, in fact, that in the first game of the series, the plate umpire, George Moriarty, had to try to control them. The big Irish umpire was offended and angered by the slurs they were spewing at Greenberg when he came to bat.

"Moriarty stopped the game in the second inning while he walked to the Cub dugout to warn manager Charlie Grimm. He said he would clear the bench if they didn't stop razzing Greenberg," the Associated Press reported.

The *New York Sun* quoted Moriarty later: "I told Grimm that if I heard any more such profanity as they yelled at Greenberg that I'd chase five of them off the bench with Grimm leading the procession."

"The language was rough," recalled Phil Cavarretta, the Cubs' young first baseman. "Detroit was on some of our players. We tried to retaliate."

"It's all in the game," Hank said afterward. "Why squawk about it now? I was a sucker to let it get my goat."

That wasn't the worst of it for Greenberg in the Series. In the second game, on a cold day in Detroit with the fans wrapped in blankets in the stands, Greenberg hit a home run in the first inning. But in the seventh, while trying to score, he collided with the Cub catcher, Gabby Hartnett, and broke his left wrist. He would be out for the rest of the Series, the Tigers going on to win it in six games without him.

For the following four games, Hank was frustrated at not being able to play. He felt like a stranger in the dugout. But the championship was still very nice, of course, and there was still another happy surprise down the line.

In late October, he received a phone call at home in the Bronx. He was told that he had just been named unanimously by the Baseball Writers Association of America as the 1935 American League Most Valuable Player.

Though his wrist was still in a cast, Hank Greenberg could hardly have been happier.

After the success of 1935, the following season was virtually a lost year for Hank in baseball. The wrist didn't respond as well as he had expected. He played in only twelve games, hitting one home run. The team suffered another setback as well. Mickey Cochrane was hit in the head with a pitch and he, too, was out for the rest of the season. The Tigers finished a distant second to the Yankees that year.

What was so different for Greenberg in 1936 was seeing a new star in the American League: Joe DiMaggio of the Yankees. He saw "Joltin' Joe," as DiMaggio would be called, as a pure natural, with a perfect stride, and a perfect swing. "He made it look so easy," said Green-

Hank Greenberg received a surprise phone call at home.

berg. DiMaggio rarely showed emotion. He was a clutch player and a smart, swift base runner. And in center field DiMaggio was so graceful it looked as if he were gliding.

By 1937, Greenberg had mended. He was eager to get back on the field and forget about the disappointing 1936 season. He also wanted to earn more than the dollar-a-year contract that he had signed. If he proved in spring training that he could play, he would get $25,000. If not, $1. This was, of course, years before the players' association was established, which would help give players in situations like Hank's the strength to bargain for a better and more secure contract.

Not only did Hank prove he could play in spring training, but he went on to have his best year ever. He hit .337, cracked 40 home runs and batted in a remarkable total of 183 runs. This was one short of the American League record held by Hank's longtime Yankee rival, Lou Gehrig. Hank believed this was his best year because he considered runs-batted-in to be the single most important offensive statistic in baseball: A team wins by scoring more runs than the opposition. And Hank loved to drive runners in.

When Charlie Gehringer, who batted ahead of Hank, came to the plate with a man on first base, Hank would yell, "Get him to third, Charlie, just get him to third. I'll get him in." It became a standing joke between them. Greenberg enjoyed telling of the time Gehringer said to him, "I suppose if I hit a double with a man on first, you'd probably trip him if he tried to go past third base."

Nineteen thirty-eight was a highly unusual year for

Greenberg. As the season rolled on, two questions seemed to be asked of him daily: When are you going to shake your slump? And, Can you break Babe Ruth's home-run record?

Though Greenberg wasn't hitting very well for average, it seemed that whenever he did get a hit, it was a home run. Hank couldn't explain it, but he admitted that he was soon aiming for the record.

By mid-July he had already hit 25 home runs and was a week or so ahead of Babe Ruth's record pace of 60 homers in 1927. "The Babe was the greatest home-run hitter we've ever had," Greenberg told a reporter, "and I really don't think I'm quite in his class. But with breaks, I might be able to get the record."

Besides trying to hit the ball, he also still had to contend with the antagonism of some rival players. In Chicago, a White Sox base runner, Joe Kuhel, sliding back to first base after a long lead off the bag, spiked Greenberg. Hank thought it was intentional and a scuffle ensued. The White Sox bench now began a vicious campaign of bench jockey directed at Greenberg.

"Someone yelled, 'Yellow Jew son of a bitch,'" recalled Eldon Auker, the Tiger pitcher. "When the ball game was over, Hank went into the White Sox clubhouse and said, 'I want the guy who called me a yellow Jew son of a bitch to get on his feet and come up here and call it to my face.' Not a guy moved. He was damn lucky, because Hank would have killed him. Hank was a tough guy."

Kuhel was fined fifty dollars by the league commissioner, and the White Sox and their manager, Jimmie Dykes, were reprimanded for "unsportsmanlike conduct and use of insulting and abusive language to members of the opposition."

Meanwhile, Hank continued to knock the ball over the fence. He had 37 homers on August 1. "Greenberg can beat the Babe's mark," said Lou Gehrig. By September 1, Greenberg's home-run total stood at 46.

Now came the really difficult part, because though he was a little ahead of the Babe's pace, Ruth in 1927 got hot and cracked 17 homers in that final month of the season. Hank would need 15 to break the record.

After one week, he still had 46. "The strain is too great," said Babe Ruth. "The boys are forever reminded about that record and it is bound to tell on them. It's telling on Greenberg now. I don't think he'll be able to make it now."

Hank was nervous about it, and the players saw him walking up and back in the dugout. But Hank still had homers in his bat. On September 23, in a doubleheader against the Indians, he hit his 55th and 56th homers. He was now three games ahead of Ruth. Hank had 56 in 145 games, Ruth 56 in 148.

In the next game, against the Browns, Hank got a couple of breaks. Hank hit a pop foul and the Browns' first baseman, George McQuinn, dropped it. Hank believed it was intentional, in order to give him another at bat. Hank then stroked a hit to right field, and he rounded the bases, got to third, and headed for home. "I thought I was out by a mile," said Hank, "but Bill McGowan, a friend of mine, was the home-plate umpire, and he called me safe." Regardless, it was homer Number 57.

Hank hit another homer over the fence and now it

Hank continued to knock the ball over the fence.

was 58 homers in 149 games, with five games left in the season.

Those next five games would be controversial. Hank got a number of walks. "They'd walk Hank," recalled Billy Rogell, the Tiger shortstop. "They didn't want him to break the record. I don't think it was just because he was Jewish but that had something to do with it." Some bigoted fans believed that it would be a terrible thing if a Jew broke one of the greatest records, if not the greatest record, in all of sports—and a record that was held by possibly the most popular athlete of all time.

Hank got a few hits in the next three games, but none were homers. On the last day of the season, the Tigers played the Indians in a doubleheader in huge Municipal Stadium in Cleveland, a very difficult place to hit a home run. It was a cloudy, cool day and Bob Feller pitched the first game for the Indians. All he did was strike out 18 batters, to establish a new record for one game. Hank struck out twice.

One game left for Hank. He needed two homers to tie the record. Not impossible, since eleven times during the season he had hit two homers in a game. In the last game of the season, Hank walked once and got three hits, all singles. It was getting darker. Finally, the plate umpire Moriarty said to Greenberg, "I'm sorry, Hank, but this is as far as I can go."

"That's all right, George," said Greenberg. "This is as far as I can go, too."

Looking back, Greenberg believed that, contrary to the legend that would grow around his pursuit of the record, he indeed received pitches to hit. He just didn't hit them over the fence. "But I was disappointed at not getting the record," said Hank. "Especially after having come so close."

As for that slump, Greenberg still managed to hit .315, and bat in 146 runs, second in the league. The Tigers, though, dropped to fourth place.

Nineteen thirty-nine was a lesser year for Greenberg in virtually every category—he batted .312, hit 33 homers, and had 112 runs batted in (second in the league to Jimmie Foxx in the latter two categories). But it was a lot better than what Lou Gehrig was going through. Gehrig, known as the Iron Horse because of his record of having played in 2,130 straight games over a period of 14 seasons, ended his streak on May 1. He was suffering from a rare, deadly disease called amyotrophic lateral sclerosis, now known as Lou Gehrig's disease, which attacks the spinal cord. Greenberg and the Tigers came to Yankee Stadium in May and saw Gehrig.

Greenberg was amazed at the sad sight of the famous ballplayer. The once-powerful man was now stooped, thin, and white-haired. He had to drag himself out of the dugout, as the Yankee captain, to present the lineup card to the umpire before the game. In two years, Gehrig would be dead, at age thirty-eight.

In 1940, Hank had a surprise waiting for him in training camp. The Tigers wanted him to try to play left field. Rudy York, a power hitter, had been their catcher for the previous two seasons, but though he was a superb hitter, York was a liability in the field. "We want Rudy in the lineup, Hank," Del Baker, the new Tiger manager said, "but he can't play anywhere else except first base."

The decision was up to Hank, since he was the all-star first baseman and, through great effort, was now one of the best fielding first basemen in the game.

But Hank knew they'd need York's bat if they were to climb into pennant contention. They had fallen to fifth place in 1939. Hank made a deal with Jack Zeller, the team general manager, who was representing Walter Briggs, the new owner. Briggs had taken control of the club when Frank Navin died in 1936. Greenberg proposed that he receive the same pay he did in 1939—forty thousand dollars—and he would try to learn left field. If he succeeded, and was the starting left-fielder on Opening Day, then he'd get a ten thousand dollar bonus. It was agreed. And Hank went about discovering the intricacies of left field the way he did everything else, with as much effort as he could possibly muster.

He had coaches hit him one fly ball after another, in order to develop the depth perception needed to judge them. He learned how to shield his eyes when the sun was glaring, and how to charge base hits. He practiced throws to the bases and to the cutoff men. He asked other outfielders how to play the caroms off the walls, and he even bought the young Tiger outfielder, Barney McCoskey, a tailor-made suit for his help. And when the season started, so did Hank—in left field.

About a week after the season was underway, a fly ball was hit to short left field. Hank thought the shortstop or the third baseman could catch it. Besides, the sun was in his eyes. The ball dropped, and two runs scored. When play was resumed, Pete Fox came out of the dugout and trotted to left field. Greenberg wondered what was going on.

"Hank," said Fox, "Baker wants me to take your place."

Hank's first reaction was to tell Fox to go back to the manager, Baker, and tell him, "No!" Hank decided against that and left the field. He went straight into the clubhouse, dressed, and hurried out of the park. Back at his hotel, Greenberg called Zeller.

"Jack," he said, "I don't want to be embarrassed again. The season just started. It was a difficult ball out there for anybody. . . . You put me in the outfield, you take your chances that I can play it. Tell Baker he'd better not pull that trick again because there was no reason to do it."

Greenberg had made his point. He was not taken out of another game. And he didn't come out not just because he had developed into an adequate outfielder, but also because he was hitting well, which was no surprise, and had led the team back into first place.

The Tigers led the second-place Indians by two games with a three-game series in Cleveland on the last weekend of the season. The Tigers had to win just one game to win the pennant. The Indians proceeded to win the first two games, and drew even. The second game of the Sunday doubleheader was the last game of the season. The Tigers, with York hitting a two-run homer, beat Cleveland and clinched the pennant by one game.

Greenberg ended the season with a .340 batting average, his best ever. He led the league in doubles, 50, home runs, 41, and runs batted in, 150. In the World Series against the Reds, Greenberg homered once, drove in 6 runs and batted .357, but the Tigers lost in seven games.

"What a disappointing lot we were coming back from Cincinnati on the train, losing the final game after a long, hard season," recalled Greenberg.

A few weeks later, though, Greenberg received some news that for him helped relieve the gloomy World Series result: He was again named the Most Valuable Player in the American League, the first man to win it twice at two positions. In 1935, he had been a first base-man. Now he was a left-fielder.

That surprise request by the Tigers in the spring, for Hank to change positions, turned out not so bad after all, for Greenberg, for York, and for the Tigers.

Hank was about to turn twenty-nine. Though he had a social life and there were always rumors in the paper that he might get married, he avoided it. "Nothing," he said, "interfered with baseball." He felt there was still time for marriage. But there was a second touchy sub-ject: women. Hank's mother had a skeptical view of some of the women. A friend and teammate with the Tigers, catcher Billy Sullivan, remembered the time in the off-season when he went home with Hank to his parents' house. A woman called for Hank, and his mother answered.

Hank's mother then called to him. He picked up the phone, but she stayed on it. Hank was trying as gently as possible to tell the woman he wasn't interested. And when she said, "After all we meant to each other, what am I going to do?" Hank's mother yelled into the phone, "Go jump in the lake!"

6

Wartime

The letter to Hank Green-
berg began: "Greetings."

This time, it wasn't from a fan or the owner of the
Tigers. It was from Uncle Sam. The United States Army
wanted Hank. He had put his name on a draft list and
was one of the first major-league players called for the
military in 1941.

There was a great deal written in the newspapers
about Hank's seeking a deferment from military service.
In fact, *Life* magazine speculated about the amount of
money Greenberg would lose by joining the army. (As
time went on, other big-name baseball players would
come under the same kind of scrutiny, most notably Ted
Williams who played through the 1942 season with the
war on.)

"It isn't as much of a sacrifice as it appears," Greenberg said at the time he was drafted. "After all, the government takes most of the fifty grand." He added, "I never asked for a deferment. I made up my mind to go when I was called. My country comes first."

Hank had been thinking more and more about this. He had only in the last couple of years begun to consider Adolf Hitler and Nazi Germany, and, of course, their treatment of Jews. "I didn't pay much attention to Hitler at first or any of the political goings-on at the time," Greenberg said. "I just went ahead and played ball. Of course, as time went by, I came to feel that if I, as a Jew, hit a home run, I was hitting one against Hitler."

It was a one-year draft (he was obligated to spend twelve months in the Army, and then would be released). Greenberg was scheduled to report on May 7. He played for Detroit until then. And on May 6, in a game against the Yankees, and, as a kind of farewell, Yankee catcher Bill Dickey whispered to Hank at his last time at bat, "Hank, we ain't gonna throw you nothin' but fastballs."

Hank swung at and missed the next three pitches, all fastballs. "I don't think Hank believed me," Dickey said years later.

Hank reported the next day as expected and became a Private First Class. His salary declined from $55,000 a year, or $11,000 a month, to $21 a month. He did his soldierly duty and even played in one baseball game. It happened that his army base had scheduled a game against a team of inmates from a Michigan prison. In the game, Hank hit a ball over the wall and out of the prison. He remembered with a laugh how the prisoners began to shout, "I'll get it! I'll get it!"

In December, Greenberg received notice that his military obligation had been shortened, and he was released. He now looked forward to getting ready for the 1941 season. But a day after his release, Sunday, December 7, 1940, Pearl Harbor, the American naval base in Hawaii, was attacked and bombed by the Japanese. The next morning the United States declared war on Japan and Germany, Japan's ally. Greenberg reenlisted.

By law, he wasn't required to serve more time in the military. He was now nearly thirty years old and beyond the age at which men were drafted. But he felt an obligation to the country. "We are in trouble," he told the Associated Press, "and there is only one thing to do— return to service." He also understood what he meant as a symbol for Jews, whom some critics said had been underrepresented in the military, then and in the past.

Greenberg switched from the infantry to the air force, received an officer's commission, and became a captain. He could have spent the war giving physical education and baseball lectures to troops in America, but he said he wanted to serve the nation overseas. And so he did, eventually participating in action with bombardier squads in India and China.

At one point, in 1943, tanks blew up at the air base in China where Greenberg was stationed. Greenberg ran for cover. Later, he said, "That was an occasion, I can assure you, when I didn't wonder whether I'd be able to return to baseball. I was quite satisfied to just be alive."

In May of 1945, Germany had surrendered, and

Greenberg's military service took him to China.

Japan would do the same in three months. On June 14, after having served a little more than four years in the military, Greenberg received his discharge papers. As he put it, he now was able to return to active duty on the baseball front.

The Tigers, who had lost the 1944 pennant to the Browns on the last day of the season, were in another race for the title. They had two new, outstanding pitchers, Dizzy Trout and Hal Newhouser, and had acquired Doc Cramer, a solid outfielder. Hank spent two weeks trying to get back into shape. His hands blistered so badly that the skin peeled off them. His legs gave him the most trouble. He couldn't seem to get back the bounce or speed in them. But, after all, he was now thirty-four years old.

"Nobody has ever attempted to resume baseball operations after so long a lapse," said the *Sporting News*.

Whitney Martin of the Associated Press wrote: "There isn't a fan or a rival player who doesn't wish for Big Hank anything but the best of luck.

"The fans wish him well because he always was a gentleman and a credit to the game, and because they admire him for his army record.

"The players are pulling for him because . . . he is a symbol of hope to all the other ballplayers in the service who fear their absence from the game might impair their effectiveness and money-earning capacity."

Hank returned to the lineup on July 1, in Detroit, and against Philadelphia. A sellout crowd of 55,000 was on hand at Briggs Stadium (the name had been changed from Navin Field) to witness the event. When Hank came to bat for the first time, they stood and gave him a tremendous ovation.

In the eighth inning, Greenberg responded in the way many had remembered him doing. He hit a home run. The crowd stood and cheered wildly again.

"Boy, it felt good to hit that one," Greenberg said after that game, which Detroit won. He also confessed that he had lain awake many nights while overseas and dreamed of one day returning to Briggs Stadium and "parking one in the left-field seats."

Despite his triumphant return, the following weeks were tough ones for Hank. He needed rest periods that he had never needed before. By August, he was batting over .300, but upon taking a day off, he said, "My legs gave out." However, he was still doing a creditable job for the Tigers, and the team came down to the end of the season neck-and-neck with Washington for the pennant.

The Tigers were playing at St. Louis on the final day of the season. There was a doubleheader scheduled. The Tigers had to win one of the two games to win the pennant. If they lost both to the Browns, who were in third place, there would be a tie with the Senators, and a one-game playoff.

It had rained heavily in St. Louis for three straight days, and the games those days had been called off. This resulted in their having to play two games in one day in order to meet the requirements of the schedule. And it rained again on this last day, Sunday, September 30. The game was delayed for fifty minutes. "Armies with mops and brooms tried to soak up the water," noted the *Detroit Free Press*. And though the bases were deep with mud, it was decided to start play. Otherwise, the season just might never end—and the World Series might never begin.

Rain fell throughout the first game. A little more than 6,000 fans showed up in a ballpark that seated over 30,000. The Browns were in the lead 4–3 when the Tigers came up in the top of the ninth. The gray afternoon was getting even darker. But the umpires refused to call the game. The first batter for Detroit, Hub Walker, singled. The next batter, Skeeter Webb, tried to bunt him over, and when the throw to second hit Walker in the back, the Tigers had two men on. The next batter sacrificed the runners over. With first base open, the

Browns chose to walk Doc Cramer to load the bases for a possible game-ending double play.

Now stepping into the batter's box, with the entire season on the line, was Hank Greenberg.

The rain continued to fall. The pitcher, Nelson Potter, threw the first pitch for a ball. The next pitch was a screwball and Greenberg saw it clearly from the moment it left Potter's hand. Hank swung and watched the ball begin to rise toward the corner of the left-field bleachers. Greenberg stood at the plate and watched the left-fielder go back, hoping the ball wouldn't hook foul or drop short.

It landed a few feet inside the foul line and over the fence. It was a grand-slam home run! The Tigers had won the pennant!

All the Tiger players ran out onto the field. They hugged and pounded Greenberg as he reached the plate.

Hank Greenberg, after four years away in military service, had indeed made it home.

In the World Series against the Cubs, Hank homered in the second game and again in the sixth. In the sixth, his blast in the eighth tied the score at 7–7. The game went into extra innings and the Cubs won, to tie the series at three games apiece. Greenberg injured his wrist in the twelfth inning while trying to hit a pitch to right field. He told no one about it except his manager, Steve O'Neill.

"For the good of the team, I'd better not play tomorrow," Greenberg told him. "I can't throw. I can't grip the bat properly, and with all it means to the rest of the players I think I should get out of the lineup."

O'Neill was uncertain what to do, and Greenberg

saw that. "I'll go in and try it," he said. "If anything goes wrong, get me out of there."

In the first inning, with runners on base, Greenberg, a slugger who rarely bunted, bunted. It surprised the Cub infield, which was playing back. All runners advanced, the Tigers scored three runs, and went on to a 9–3 win and the World Series championship.

After the season, Hank continued a romantic relationship that he had begun in 1944 while still in the military. Through mutual friends, he had met Caral Gimbel, the dark-haired daughter of Bernard Gimbel, president and one of the principal owners of the Gimbel Brothers and Saks Fifth Avenue department stores. She thought he was handsome and "with a divine sense of humor."

Caral Gimbel would always remember the first time Hank asked her for a date. She accepted. "You don't have to feel pinned down to this," he said to her. "If something comes up that you would rather do, then we can switch it. Call me." She had never had anyone ask her to dinner and then say that. She thought it was remarkable.

Nothing "came up" for Caral that night. They went out, and continued to.

They were from two different worlds. Hank was the son of immigrant parents who spoke English with an accent and, though financially comfortable, were hardly rich. The Gimbels were now very assimilated Jewish-Americans who lived a grand life-style. They enjoyed great wealth and large homes with servants and butlers and riding stables in Connecticut and Florida. Hank played baseball. Caral rode show horses. Hank knew about Casey Stengel. Caral knew about Stravinsky. Yet, Hank and Caral fell in love.

In the winter after the World Series, they decided to get married. In February of 1946, while driving to Florida for Hank to join the Tigers in spring training, the couple stopped off in a small town in Georgia. There they enlisted a justice of the peace and, with a handful of local people as witnesses, exchanged marriage vows.

The season started slowly for Greenberg, and he felt the years had taken their toll, especially in his legs. He was thirty-five years old, relatively advanced for a big-league baseball player. He had also never felt that he had gotten back his "baseball legs"—the spring he once felt in them—after his tour of duty in the military. Hank was having a little harder time with the pitchers, as well, and felt his reactions were slow. He began talking about retirement. This talk was hastened by the periodic boos from, of all people, some Detroit fans. He was even booed in fielding practice when a ball went through his legs. When Caral heard this, she would wince. Hank didn't like the boos, either, but said, "It's all part of the day's work."

Yet he continued to hit the ball fairly solidly, and in September he really got hot. The old bones were responding again. He passed Ted Williams in runs batted in and in homers and led the league in both, with 127 and 44 respectively. Williams finished with 38 homers and 123 RBIs. For Greenberg, at age thirty-five, it was some feat: Not only to lead the league, but to beat out Ted Williams who, Greenberg believed, "was the best hitter of my time."

Meanwhile, Greenberg played 142 games at first base,

which was a decent amount, but fewer than at any time when he was healthy and with a team all season. There were two other baseball signs of advanced age: Hank's batting average dropped to .277, and he led the league in errors with 15.

At the end of the season, a disagreement developed between Walter Briggs, the owner of the Tigers, and Greenberg. Briggs seemed to believe that Hank was unhappy with Detroit and perhaps wanted to return to his hometown, New York. Hank had never said that. Hank wondered, though, if Briggs were just making up an excuse to get rid of him. He would then not have to pay an aging ballplayer the kind of money Hank was making, and he might demand even more, especially after having led the league in homers and RBIs.

Then one day in January of the following year, 1947, Hank, listening to radio, heard an amazing thing: He had been sold to the Pittsburgh Pirates! He was shocked, disappointed, and then angry. After all the years of good service with Detroit, it should come to this, he thought, that not only should Detroit sweep him aside, but not even have the courtesy to tell him directly.

Greenberg decided to retire from baseball. He felt too bitter about the game to continue in it. Besides all this, he and Caral also had a baby on the way, due in late January. It was about time he quit as a player, he figured, and get into some kind of business. Over the years he had developed friendships with numerous influential business people.

One man took a different view about whether Hank should retire from baseball. That man was John Galbreath, the new and wealthy owner of the Pirates. He wanted Hank because he believed Greenberg would lend some credibility to a poor team and perhaps give a winner's attitude to it. He phoned Hank to tell him he was coming to New York and suggested they have dinner. Hank told him there was no chance he would return to baseball, but he would be happy to have dinner with him anyway.

"Mr. Galbreath," Hank said, when they sat down in the restaurant, "I just don't want to play anymore. I can't travel on trains. I get a kink in my neck."

"Hank," said Galbreath, "we'll fly you."

"I'm older. I don't like having a roommate on the road."

"We'll get you your own room."

"And Forbes Field is a big ballpark down the left-field line." The distance from home plate to left was 365 feet.

"How far is it in Briggs Stadium?"

"Three hundred and forty feet."

"We'll move in the fences to three forty," said Galbreath. "We'll build a bullpen there."

"Well, what are you willing to pay?" asked Greenberg.

"You'll get paid whatever you want."

Greenberg thought for a moment. Things had been going fairly well up to now, but he still really didn't want to play. He threw out a figure well above anything any other player was making.

"I'd want one hundred thousand dollars," said Greenberg.

"You got it," said Galbreath.

So Hank Greenberg played one more season, and he had an attractive, and closer, left-field fence to look at. That area was dubbed "Greenberg's Gardens."

The Pirates were an awful team, and the players generally seemed devoid of any winning feeling. The atmosphere was totally unlike Hank's Detroit years. The best player the Pirates had was a twenty-four-old named Ralph Kiner, who had led the National League in homers the year before, his rookie season, with 23.

Kiner and Greenberg took an immediate liking to each other and developed a nearly father-son relationship. Hank not only showed Ralph how to hit and adjust his swing for greater power, he even helped him pick out his street clothes.

Hank began the season in an unusual way. It wasn't so much that he lashed a double to drive in the only run of the game, as the Pirates beat the Cubs 1–0. It was that the Pirate pitcher he won the game for was none other than Rip Sewell, with whom, thirteen years earlier, he had had a fight in spring training over what Greenberg perceived as anti-Semitic remarks by Sewell.

Sewell, when they met again with the Pirates, said, "Henry, you know you and I had a fight. You know that you and I have grown up. We've become men instead of kids."

Greenberg decided to "ley bygones be bygones." Now that they were teammates, Hank decided that there would be no purpose to continue any hostility.

While Greenberg was having a decent, though not a great start, Kiner was terrible. After about a month, and despite the closer left-field fence, Kiner had hit only three home runs. The top echelon of the Pirates, including the manager, wanted to send him to the minor leagues to try to restore his confidence and his batting eye.

"Don't do it," Greenberg told them. "Keep Ralph Kiner with the team. I'll take him as a roommate. He and I will get along great, and I'm sure I can help him. I'm sure he'll put in a good performance."

The Pirates kept Kiner, who went on to hit 51 homers for the season, leading the major leagues. He also went on to lead the National League in home-run hitting five more times—seven straight years, in fact, including 1946 and 1947—for which he was elected to the Hall of Fame in 1975. And when Hank retired, "Greenberg's Gardens" became known as "Kiner's Korner."

Meanwhile, in early May, the Brooklyn Dodgers came to Pittsburgh with their famous rookie, Jackie Robinson. He was the first black man in modern times to play in the major leagues. There was a great deal of attention paid to Robinson, because a number of people felt that blacks shouldn't be playing ball with whites. This was at a time when segregation was law in many parts of the United States. There, blacks had to go to separate schools. They were forced to use separate public facilities, such as washrooms and drinking fountains. In many ballparks, blacks even had to sit in a separate section, one that was generally in the sun; the whites sat in the shade.

Robinson received death threats regularly. It is believed that he dodged more pitches at the plate and more spikings on the bases than anyone else. But he continued to go about his business of trying to contribute to his team. He played first base that year and was a good hitter and an exceptional and daring base runner.

Hank was interested in seeing him. And what he saw, as he later described it," was a man like a black prince, with grace and dignity." Some fans and some of the players in Greenberg's own dugout called out to Robinson, "Hey, coal mine, hey coal mine, hey you black coal mine, we're going to get you! You ain't gonna play no baseball!"

Greenberg remembered what it had been like for him. To a reporter's question, Hank said: "The more they ride him the more they will spur him on. It threw me a lot when I first came up. I know how he feels."

After that first game, on May 17, a headline in The New York Times read: HANK GREENBERG A HERO TO DODGERS' NEGRO STAR.

This was the story behind that headline, as reported by the Associated Press:

Jackie Robinson, first Negro player in the major leagues, had picked a diamond hero—rival first baseman Hank Greenberg of the Pittsburgh Pirates.

Here's why: Robinson and Greenberg collided in a play at first base during the current Pirate-Dodger series. The next time Jackie came down to the sack, Hank said, "I forgot to ask you if you were hurt in that play."

Assured that Robinson was unharmed, Greenberg said: "Stick in there. You're doing fine. Keep your chin up."

This encouragement from an established star heartened Robinson, who has been the subject of antiracial treatment elsewhere and admits he has undergone "jockeying—some of it pretty severe."

"Class tells. It sticks out all over Mr. Greenberg," Robinson declared.

Greenberg said to Robinson, "Stick in there. You're doing fine."

For Greenberg, there was nothing more to say on the matter. His actions spoke for him.

The season overall wasn't much fun for Hank. The team ended up in last place, and his play was not up to his standards. He had promised Galbreath, the Pirate owner, that he would hit at least 25 home runs, more than any Pirate had ever hit, and indeed hit exactly 25. But he played in only 125 games, and his batting average and runs-batted-in totals were at career lows of .249 and 74 RBIs.

He was also hurting physically. His legs were aching and he had a bad arm. There were bone chips in his right elbow that had to be operated on. It was time now, Hank decided, to retire. He had promised Galbreath one season, and he wouldn't be talked into any more.

A month after the season, he received a letter from Galbreath, which said, "I want to say, Hank, that you fulfilled every promise you made. No one could have tried any harder or given any more time and effort to try to earnestly carry out every letter of a contract than you did."

The letter not only summed up Greenberg's season at Pittsburgh, it seemed to sum up his entire baseball career, and everything else Hank became involved in. "Looking back," Hank said, "I played hard. I tried my best."

7

Hall of Fame

Nine years after Hank retired as an active player, he was elected to the Baseball Hall of Fame. The induction ceremony, which also included Joe Cronin, the former great Red Sox shortstop, was held on a Sunday in August of 1956. Hank stood in the sun in a suit, the wind blowing his hair a little, and held the plaque that would be hung on the wall in the Cooperstown pantheon.

The plaque noted that Hank was "one of baseball's greatest right-handed batters," which then included such players as Rogers Hornsby, Jimmie Foxx, and Joe DiMaggio. The plaque mentioned Greenberg's home-run and runs-batted-in records, the World Series and All-Star Games he played in, and the grandslam that won the pennant on the last day of the 1945 season. It

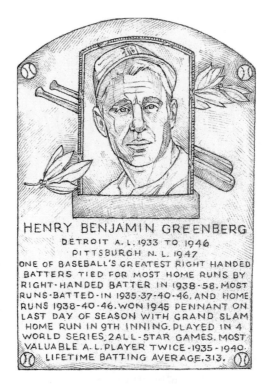

HENRY BENJAMIN GREENBERG
DETROIT A. L. 1933 TO 1946
PITTSBURGH N. L. 1947
ONE OF BASEBALL'S GREATEST RIGHT HANDED
BATTERS TIED FOR MOST HOME RUNS BY
RIGHT-HANDED BATTER IN 1938-58. MOST
RUNS-BATTED-IN 1935-37-40-46, AND HOME
RUNS 1938-40-46. WON 1945 PENNANT ON
LAST DAY OF SEASON WITH GRAND SLAM
HOME RUN IN 9TH INNING. PLAYED IN 4
WORLD SERIES, 2 ALL-STAR GAMES. MOST
VALUABLE A. L. PLAYER TWICE-1935-1940.
LIFETIME BATTING AVERAGE. 313.

The Hall of Fame plaque

noted his two Most Valuable Player awards and said that he finished his career with a .313 batting average.

It couldn't say everything, of course. It didn't say that, when he retired, he was third behind Babe Ruth and Jimmie Foxx in home-run percentage. And the plaque didn't reflect that he had homered in 6.4 percent of his official at bats. Or that he was tied for first with Sam Thompson and Lou Gehrig for highest average of runs batted in per game, at .925, just ahead of Joe Di-Maggio, Ruth, Foxx and Ted Williams.

It didn't say, naturally, about the sweat, the thought, the striving, the practice, the dedication, the dreaming, and the guts that it had taken Hank to accomplish all that.

But Hank spoke for himself, as he always had.

"In all my years of being on the playing field I never dreamed that this would be the final result," he told the press. "I can't possibly express how I feel. It's just too wonderful for words. I'm deeply grateful and humble for this honor.

"I've had many thrills in baseball," he added. "This, though, is the greatest. Today I have the same butterflies in my stomach that I used to have when I came to the plate with the bases full with Grove or Gomez or Ruffing pitching."

By this time, in 1956, Greenberg was the general manager of the Cleveland Indians. After his playing career ended, he wasn't quite sure what avenue to pursue. He had saved about $300,000 from his playing days—a great amount, especially considering that he had earned $447,000 in total from playing professional baseball. So he wasn't in a rush to do anything. Then he met Bill Veeck, at that time the flamboyant owner of the Indians. Hank immediately became attracted to Veeck, with his knowledge of a variety of subjects—baseball being just one.

In fact, when they first met at the World Series of 1947, Veeck began talking about how disgracefully the Indians had been treated. It took Greenberg a little while to realize he was talking about American Indians, and not the Cleveland Indians. It was Veeck who hired the first black player in the American League. Larry

Doby, a second baseman and later an outfielder, joined the Indians in June of 1947, two months after Jackie Robinson broke in with the Dodgers in the National League.

Veeck also brought forty-two-year-old Satchel Paige, the star pitcher in the Negro Leagues, to the Indians in 1948. Some thought it was a stunt. Veeck had been known for his controversial or imaginative promotional ideas. (In fact, the most famous of his career was to come three years later when Veeck, then the owner of the Browns, put a midget into a game. The midget walked on four pitches, and a pinch runner replaced him at first base.) However, Satchel Paige contributed to a winning team, with an 8–3 pitching record that season.

Veeck was a man with great humor and self-confidence. When he had part of his leg amputated because of complications from a war injury, he threw a party shortly after and danced on his new peg leg. Bill Veeck refused to feel sorry for himself. This was a man Hank Greenberg could relate to and enjoy.

When Veeck invited Greenberg to join the Cleveland Indians organization, to own a part of the team, and to learn the business from the other side of the playing field, Greenberg said yes.

In 1948, the Indians not only won the pennant and the World Series, but set an all-time baseball attendance record at home by drawing more than two million people. "Bill Veeck," said Greenberg, "is the Pied Piper of baseball."

Greenberg just observed Veeck that first year. Then he earned more responsibilities and became the head of the farm system. When Veeck left in 1949 to become owner of the St. Louis Browns, Greenberg became general manager of the Indians.

While this was going on, Hank and Caral were having marital difficulties. Their worlds, vastly different to begin with, seemed to grow even further apart. She still didn't relate to baseball as fully as Hank would have liked, and Hank never grew deeply involved with her life of museums and country clubs and horse riding.

Hank's professional concentration remained baseball, to be sure. During his reign as general manager, the Indians were always a contending team. They won a pennant under Greenberg in 1954, though they lost the World Series to the New York Giants in a disappointing four straight games. It was a series in which the Indians flopped despite having one of the most highly regarded pitching staffs in World Series history, including two 23-game winners, Bob Lemon and Early Wynn; a 19-game winner, Mike Garcia; and Bob Feller, who though in the twilight of his career still finished with a 13–3 record.

It also was the series in which Dusty Rhodes hit two dramatic pinch-hit homers for the Giants. Willie Mays, the Giants' young centerfielder, made one of the most spectacular catches in baseball history, to rob Vic Wertz of a long hit and save significant runs in the first game.

One of the stars of the Indians at this time was Al Rosen, the third baseman and a Jew. Rosen, who grew up in Miami, Florida, had idolized Greenberg and was thrilled to join the team that Greenberg was now associated with. They had dinner together and Hank told him to "ignore the bigots and just play to the best of your ability." It was the same advice that Hank had received from Moe Berg, the veteran Jewish catcher, when Hank was a young player.

"I'm sure that even later after I played, there were other Jewish ballplayers . . . there was Sandy Koufax, for example, one of the greatest pitchers who ever threw, and a Hall of Famer, and I'm sure he had problems," Rosen said years later. "As you get older you shrug those problems off. You're not as quick to react to them.

"I always felt I had to conduct myself—and I'm sure Hank felt the same way—in a courtly manner," Rosen would say, "and I wanted people to think of me in a certain frame of mind, a certain way. Dignity is the word I'm searching for."

Greenberg and Rosen were friendly and socialized occasionally in the evenings with their wives and other friends. They regularly played racquetball together. Yet, as time went on, Rosen and Greenberg had disagreements that drew them apart. Rosen felt that Greenberg seemed to expect more out of him than he did other players, and though they were friendly an antagonism developed. Rosen wasn't sure why and wondered if there was some subconscious jealousy on Hank's part— Rosen questioned whether Hank felt that Rosen was the Jew in Cleveland baseball receiving accolades while Greenberg was often being criticized in the press for his handling of the team. Even though the Indians were invariably in the pennant race, there was also a certain amount of sniping at them by the press.

One day Rosen went to Greenberg to try to get a bonus of $5,000.

"Remember," said Hank, "we gave you a $5,000 bonus."

"Well, if you're going to talk about bonuses," said Rosen, "what about my moving from third base to first? In 1940, you moved from first base to left field for $10,000."

"Yes," said Hank, "but that was me and this is you."

Rosen said later: "Hank could be very tough."

Hank was not always diplomatic with reporters either and was a sharp contrast in this area to Bill Veeck. Hank was quicker to anger, quicker to tell a reporter that the man simply didn't know what he was talking about.

After having won the pennant in 1954, the Indians finished second the following two seasons. But in 1957 they dropped to sixth place in the American League. Hank took the brunt of the blame from fans and the press. And the Indians fired him as their general manager.

In 1959, Veeck bought the Chicago White Sox and sought his pal Greenberg to join him. Hank, who had begun to establish a stock-investment company in New York, hesitated, but he couldn't resist going back into business with a guy he loved, respected, and admired. Hank became the vice president of the White Sox. In Veeck's and Greenberg's first year there, 1959, the White Sox won the pennant for the first time in 40 years.

Veeck left the Sox after a few years, and Greenberg became the general manager for one year. But he couldn't give it his entire attention because he had become a weekend father.

A few years earlier, while still living in Cleveland, he

and Caral had been divorced. Their three children, sons Glenn and Stephen and daughter Alva, their youngest, were living in New York. The joint custody agreement allowed that the children would stay with Hank during the school year. So he had a housekeeper look after them during the week—Caral, who lived a few blocks away, looked in on them as well—while he would fly from Chicago to New York to be with them on weekends.

The commute became difficult, and Hank soon decided to leave baseball and move permanently to Manhattan.

The boys grew up hearing baseball legends about their father. Glenn, the oldest, was born in his father's last year as a ballplayer. His sons were therefore more impressed with him as the general manager of the Indians and White Sox than they were of Hank as a ballplayer. His role as general manager was current, it carried stature in their school, and they got into the baseball games free and had good seats.

They would always remember stories their father told of how, when other players were out chasing women, he was out chasing fly balls. How, as the season wore on and other players, especially the pitchers, got weaker, he got stronger. He told them that he always felt that getting his rest at night, instead of hanging out in bars as many players did, kept him in the best shape possible.

Hank could also be competitive with his children, challenging them with questions about what they learned in school. Then, when both boys went to Yale and came home using rather large words, Hank, who

Hank Greenberg and his three children

had gone only one semester to college, would say, "Oh, so now you're an expert!"

But Hank didn't pressure either of the boys in sports, and both appreciated it. Sometimes they found it difficult to be a son of Hank Greenberg, since there were certain athletic expectations. However, these were not overwhelming.

Besides, they took pride in their father's achievements. Glenn played soccer on his prep school soccer team. One day his father came to see a game. The ball bounced to the sidelines where he stood. Hank, who hadn't been around a soccer ball since he made all-city in that sport in high school, booted the ball back onto the field. Glenn remembers his amazement. He had never seen anyone kick a ball that far before.

Glenn preferred football to baseball simply because he was better at it. He became a football player at Yale, a lineman. In later years he was also a nationally ranked amateur racquetball player. Stephen was an all-American soccer goalie at Yale and then became a professional baseball player, getting as high as Triple A ball. When he realized that his chances of becoming a major leaguer of substance was dim, he decided, with the encouragement of his father, to go to law school.

Strangely enough, for the children of the great Jewish baseball hero, they received very little Jewish instruction. Their mother did not have conventional Jewish ties to the community, and their father had drifted from it. In some ways, he had tossed off the mantle of the Jewish hero. Now, out of the limelight, he felt a relief from the responsibility of being a Jew, a responsibility that he had carried with so much dignity for so long.

Also, he felt that there was a distinction between being a Jew and being a religious person. He was skeptical of organized religion, being cynical towards zealotry of any fashion, but remained a proud Jew.

"If there really was a true religion," Hank said, "it should bring people together, or at least that's what I've always thought. God loves everybody and we're all the children of God. As a matter of fact, at an early age I took the Ten Commandments as my code of living. I'm satisfied that I've tried to live up to the Ten Commandments."

Meanwhile, the children did not grow up going to temple. Nor were any of them confirmed in the traditional manner, by becoming bar mitzvah, or in Alva's case, bat mitzvah. Rarely did they have a Jewish holiday dinner, and there was virtually no discussion of Judaism in the household.

Stephen recalls a day in early October of 1959, when the boys were thirteen and eleven, and Alva was with their mother: "We got up to go to school. My dad said, 'You're not going to school today.'"

"We asked why not? He said, 'I'm taking you someplace.'"

"'Why dad?'"

"'Because this is Yom Kippur.'"

"'What's that?'"

"'This is the holiest day in the year—it's the day of atonement for the Jews. You're not going to school today.'" Terrific! we thought.

"My brother and I got dressed. And we went to the Hayden Planetarium. I had never been there before. We spent two or three hours there. Traditionally, on Yom

Kippur, Jews fast and stay in synagogue, but we didn't. Jews ask for forgiveness for all their sins of the past year, the slate is wiped clean, and they start a new year making vows to be better the next year. And to reinforce that, you don't eat. I came home and I distinctly remember that I felt real good. It was a great day. But it was several years before I realized that Yom Kippur was not a day that Jews went to the planetarium.

"What else would I think? He's not going to take us to temple, because he doesn't believe in that. He took us some place that was obviously special. Some place that maybe represented the vast unknown; someplace he hadn't been for a long time. It was for him a reaching out halfway or three quarters of the way back to something, but he couldn't go all the way.

"But he wanted to do something. And that's what he came up with. It was going someplace peaceful and thinking about what you've done in the last year, how you might do differently or better next year, and without the supposed trappings of religion."

Hank remained in the stock-investment business and made a great deal of money, enough so that he could have retired and lived comfortably at any time. Meanwhile, he still watched baseball. He took an interest in several players, but none more than Sandy Koufax. "Did Dad follow Koufax's career because he was Jewish? I'm sure it was a factor," his son Stephen once said.

Hank always remained conscious of his role as a Jewish ballplayer. He continued to ponder the hero-worship he had received.

"People remember that I didn't play on Yom Kippur. They remember it every year, but in fact the situation arose only once, in 1934.

"It's a strange thing. When I was playing I used to resent being singled out as a Jewish ballplayer, period. I'm not sure why or when I changed, because I'm still not a particularly religious person. Lately, though, I find myself wanting to be remembered not only as a great ballplayer, but even more as a great *Jewish* ballplayer."

In fact, the topic of Jews and Israel led to a rift between Hank and his son Glenn. Glenn had married a gentile woman and at dinner one evening she took a pro-Palestinian view in their discussion. Hank took the Israeli view and an argument ensued. It led to a separation between father and son that lasted five years. Hank gave much of his charitable contributions to Jewish causes, and assumed that Catholics did for Catholics and Protestants for Protestants. It turned out that only through intercessions from Stephen, Alva, and Hank's new wife, Mary Jo, did Hank and Glenn finally heal the breach.

Hank and Mary Jo met at a game during the 1959 World Series between the Dodgers and Hank's team, the White Sox. Soon after, they met again in New York, at a lunch with mutual friends. Mary Jo DeCicco was a tall, striking blonde who had been a movie starlet. She had appeared in a couple of westerns and one "A" film, *An Affair with a Stranger,* as the third lead behind Victor Mature and Jean Simmons. She had been discovered when the film producer Howard Hughes saw her as a teenager while at a movie theater in Tucson, Arizona.

After a while she left show business. "I was never really interested in it," she said. "And I was never comfortable with it. I was satisfied with my life and had no desire for a career. Hank saw my films and said I was a fool to quit. He thought I had a lot of talent, and all I had to do was work at it. He said, 'You're a natural.' But it simply wasn't for me."

The couple first lived in Manhattan. Then, in 1974, when Hank was sixty-three, they moved to Beverly Hills and a new life style. He regularly saw Stephen, now a lawyer, who lived in Los Angeles. Glenn was a stockbroker back in Manhattan, and Alva had bought part of a small newspaper in Connecticut. All had married, and Hank had become a grandfather several times over.

Hank swam in the pool in his home. He continued checking the stock market, still invested, but his main interest now was playing tennis. Interestingly, he played a softer, more strategic kind of tennis than the power game one might have expected from the former baseball slugger. Hank loved tennis and was good at it and a ferocious competitor, which came as no surprise to people who knew him.

He was competitive with friends, with his sons and daughter—with anyone, in fact, who played with him. "The only thing worse than playing against Hank in tennis," Ralph Kiner, his friend through the years, once recalled with a smile, "was playing with him in doubles. He was really demanding."

And Hank was having a great time with his life. There were family, friends, parties, books, laughs, thoughtful discussions on a variety of subjects, tennis, a plump bank account, and the California sunshine. Then suddenly much of his idyllic world changed.

8

Final Days

In the fall of 1985, Green-
berg was diagnosed as having cancer of the kidney.
There was a chance he could beat it—he was sure he
could. He told only his immediate family about his disease. He wanted no sympathy, no accounts in the newspapers. This was his quiet fight. "He figured he'd win—
it was like facing Bob Feller and then hitting a home
run—and then he'd tell everybody that he did it," said
Stephen.

In January of 1986, Hank learned that his good friend
Bill Veeck, one of the dearest people in his life, had
died. On the phone with a caller, the day after the
death, Hank told this story about him:

"Years ago, when Bill was single, he was enamoured
of a young dancer. At one point, she was traveling from
New York to Los Angeles on the train, the Twentieth
Century Limited, and the train made frequent stops.

Bill had a florist meet the train at every stop and deliver a basket of roses to this young lady. When she finally arrived at the California station, it looked like she came with a flower shop. But that was Bill's idea of charming a lady."

When Hank finished the story, he laughed, but one also heard in his voice the deep emotion he felt for his departed friend.

Hank wasn't getting much healthier. He tried. He did everything the doctors told him, but he seemed to get weaker. He couldn't move about the house much, and he couldn't even speak for long periods without becoming exhausted.

One day, talking with Stephen at Hank's home, Hank broke down in tears. It was a deeply emotional moment for Stephen. He had never seen his father cry. He had always known him as a great, strong man who, it seemed, would be strong forever.

Mary Jo suffered along with Hank on a minute-by-minute basis. When Hank had surgery shortly after learning of the cancer, he wrote letters to Stephen and Mary Jo that he said they should open if he didn't make it. He told both how proud he was of them, and how happy they had made him. He wrote to Mary Jo:

Remember, I said, "Shed no tear for me." I've had a wonderful life, filled with personal success and blessed with very good health. Plus, wonderful children who have never caused me a moment's concern. They have brought only joy and pride in their accomplishments.

Most importantly I shared the last twenty-five years with you, and that's more than any man is entitled to.

And so my love, we will meet again somewhere, sometime.

Your husband and sweetheart. xxx Hank.

Henry Benjamin Greenberg

The pain for Hank in the late summer of 1986 was excruciating. He hobbled about on crutches, and hoped and fought to return to health. It was not to be. At 8:50 on Thursday morning, September 4, Henry Benjamin Greenberg died in his sleep. He was seventy-five years old.

Greenberg's death was news all across the country. It was in headlines, and it was on the network broadcasts.

People recalled his kindness, his strength, his baseball prowess. About a month after his death, a memorial service for him was held in a small theater in Los Angeles. About 300 people attended, including friends, family and well-wishers. A handful of close friends spoke about him. His son Stephen was the last speaker and perhaps summed up for everyone the life of his father.

"He was my mentor, my best friend, and, yes, my favorite doubles partner," said Stephen. "He taught me many lessons that I will carry with me forever. But, most of all, he taught me that you don't have to break every record to achieve greatness, you don't have to be invincible to be strong, and you don't have to be perfect to be loved."

STATISTICS

HENRY BENJAMIN GREENBERG
"Hank"
Born January 1, 1911, New York, NY
Batted and threw right-handed
Height: 6'3½"   Weight: 210 lbs.

Year	Team	League	Position	Games	At Bats	Runs Scored	Hits	Doubles	Triples	Home Runs	Runs Batted In	Batting Average	Put Outs	Fielding Average
1930–Hartford	East.	1B	17	56	10	12	1	2	2	6	.214	157	.988
1930–Raleigh	Pied.	1B	122	452	88	142	26	14	19	93	.314	1052	.980
1930–Detroit	Amer.	1B	1	1	0	0	0	0	0	0	.000	0	.000
1931–Evansville	I.I.I.	1B	126	487	88	155	**41**	10	15	85	.318	**1248**	.982
1931–Beaumont	Texas	PH	3	2	0	0	0	0	0	0	.000	0	.000
1932–Beaumont	Texas	1B	154	600	**123**	174	31	11	**39**	131	.290	1437	.989
1933–Detroit	Amer.	1B	117	449	59	135	33	3	12	87	.301	1133	.988
1934–Detroit	Amer.	1B	153	593	118	201	**63**	7	26	139	.339	1454	.990
1935–Detroit	Amer.	1B	152	619	121	203	46	16	**36**	**170**	.328	1437	.992
1936–Detroit	Amer.	1B	12	46	10	16	6	2	1	16	.348	119	.992
1937–Detroit	Amer.	1B	154	594	137	200	49	14	40	**183**	.337	**1477**	.992
1938–Detroit	Amer.	1B	155	556	**144**	175	23	4	**58**	146	.315	**1484**	.991
1939–Detroit	Amer.	1B	138	500	112	156	42	7	33	112	.312	1205	**.993**
1940–Detroit	Amer.	OF	148	573	129	195	**50**	8	**41**	**150**	.340	298	.954
1941–Detroit	Amer.	OF	19	67	12	18	5	1	2	12	.269	32	.914
1942/43/44–Detroit	Amer.		(In Military Service)											
1945–Detroit	Amer.	OF	78	270	47	84	20	2	13	60	.311	129	1.000
1946–Detroit	Amer.	1B	142	523	91	145	29	5	**44**	**127**	.277	1272	.989
1947–Pittsburgh	Nat.	1B	125	402	71	100	13	2	25	74	.249	983	.992
Major League Totals				1394	5193	1051	1628	379	71	331	1276	.313	11023	.990

WORLD SERIES RECORD

Year	Team	League	Position	Games	At Bats	Runs Scored	Hits	Doubles	Triples	Home Runs	Runs Batted In	Batting Average	Put Outs	Fielding Average
1934–Detroit	Amer.	1B	7	28	4	9	2	1	1	7	.321	60	.985
1935–Detroit	Amer.	1B	2	6	1	1	0	0	1	2	.167	17	.864
1940–Detroit	Amer.	OF	7	28	5	10	2	1	1	6	.357	12	1.000
1945–Detroit	Amer.	OF	7	23	7	7	3	0	2	7	.304	8	1.000
World Series Totals				23	85	17	27	7	2	5	22	.318	97	.963

Bold face type indicates league leader

Adapted from *Hank Greenberg: The Story of My Life*, edited and with an introduction by Ira Berkow (New York: Times Books, 1989), p. 292.

IMPORTANT DATES

1911 Hank Greenberg born in Greenwich Village,
     New York City, on January 11.

1917 Moved to the Bronx.

1929 Graduated from James Monroe High School.
     Entered New York University.
     Signed a professional baseball contract with the
      Detroit Tigers.

1930 Dropped out of NYU.
     Began professional career by joining Hartford,
      CT of the Eastern League.
     Was sent to Raleigh, NC of the Piedmont
      League.
     Came up to the Tigers at the end of the season.

1931–32 In minor leagues, with Evansville, IL and Beau-
     mont, TX.

1933 Joins Tigers, becomes a regular first baseman.

1934 Becomes one of the stars of the pennant-
     winning Tigers.

1935 Bats in 170 runs and is named Most Valuable
     Player in the American League. In World

Series, the Chicago Cubs are reprimanded by umpire George Moriarty for ethnic slurs at Greenberg.

Breaks left wrist in second game of World Series.

1936   Breaks same wrist, plays only 12 games in the season.

1937   Drives in 183 runs, misses by one run the American League record held by Lou Gehrig.

1938   Hits 58 home runs and misses by two the major-league record held by Babe Ruth.

1939   Starts at first base for the American League in the All-Star game.

1940   Moves to left field, is named American League MVP for the second time, and the first player to be honored with this award at two different positions (he was a first baseman in 1934). The Tigers also play in the pennant, but lose the World Series to the Cincinnati Reds.

1941   In May is drafted into the army.
In December is released. But reinlists a day later, Dec. 7, when Pearl Harbor is bombed.

1942–44   Serves as captain in air force in China and India.

1945   Discharged from military, joins Tigers in July. Hits home run with bases loaded on last day of season to help them win the pennant.
Tigers beat Cubs in the World Series.

1946   Greenberg and Caral Gimbel are married.
Greenberg leads American League in home runs and runs batted in, beating out Ted Williams for both honors.

1947   The Greenbergs' first son, Glenn, is born.
Is sent by Tigers to Pirates in a cash deal. He befriends young players Ralph Kiner and Jackie Robinson. He retires as an active player at age thirty-six after this season.

1948   Joins Cleveland Indians as an executive under Bill Veeck.
Cleveland wins the pennant.

1949	Stephen, the Greenbergs' second son, is born. Greenberg becomes general manager of the Indians.
1954	The Greenbergs' third and last child, a daughter, Alva, is born. Indians win pennant under Greenberg.
1956	Elected to the Baseball Hall of Fame.
1957	Greenberg is dismissed as general manager of the Indians.
1958	Caral and Hank Greenberg get divorced
1959	Greenberg becomes vice-president of the Chicago White Sox under Veeck. White Sox win the pennant.
1961–63	Becomes general manager of the White Sox.
1964	Becomes a full-time stock investor.
1966	Greenberg weds Mary Jo DeCicco.
1974	Greenbergs move from New York City to Beverly Hills, California.
1983	Is named honorary captain of the American League all-star team.
1986	Hank Greenberg dies, at age seventy-five, on September 4.

INDEX